The Origin of the Hebrews and Their Faith

The Origin of the Hebrews and Their Faith

Aaron Tomer

WIPF & STOCK · Eugene, Oregon

THE ORIGIN OF THE HEBREWS AND THEIR FAITH

Copyright © 2019 Aaron Tomer. All rights reserved. Except for brief quotations in critical publications or reviews, no part of this book may be reproduced in any manner without prior written permission from the publisher. Write: Permissions, Wipf and Stock Publishers, 199 W. 8th Ave., Suite 3, Eugene, OR 97401.

Wipf & Stock
An Imprint of Wipf and Stock Publishers
199 W. 8th Ave., Suite 3
Eugene, OR 97401

www.wipfandstock.com

PAPERBACK ISBN: 978-1-5326-8653-5
HARDCOVER ISBN: 978-1-5326-8654-2
EBOOK ISBN: 978-1-5326-8655-9

Manufactured in the U.S.A. SEPTEMBER 6, 2019

Figure II.1, Reproduced by permission of www.BibleLandPictures.com / Alamy Stock Photo.

Figure III.1, Reproduced by kind permission of the Wellcome Library, London.

Figure III.2, © The Trustees of the British Museum.

Figure IV.1 and A.2, © The Trustees of the British Museum.

Figure IV.2, Reproduced by kind permission of the Wellcome Library, London.

Figure V.2, © The Trustees of the British Museum.

Figure A.1, Reproduced by kind permission of the Wellcome Library, London. Other figures, of public domains or the author.

"God is One, alone and none other existeth; He is not to be seen in a sculptured image, thou canst not conceive his form in thy heart" (EGYPTIAN PAPYRUS, 4700 BC).

Contents

Preface / ix

Chapter I	The Origin of the Hebrews / 1	
Chapter II	Exodus—Myth and Reality / 24	
Chapter III	The Settlement in the Land of Canaan / 50	
Chapter IV	Moses and the Hebrew Theology / 84	
Chapter V	The Development and Sublimation of the Jewish Monotheism / 96	

Appendix / 107
The Papyrus of Hor / 108
Chronicle / 110
Bibliography / 113

Preface

THIS BOOK IS DEDICATED to the reader who is interested in the origin of the Hebrew nation and its culture, as they are reflected in the study of the Hebrew writings themselves, the Hebrew Bible, historical documentation, and archeological findings.

The book discusses the origin of the Patriarchs, Abraham, Isaac, and Jacob, and of the Mothers; the origin of the twelve tribes and relating them to one family; their integration in the land of Canaan, and their adoption of a new God.

The book describes the conquest of the land and the establishment of the kingdom based on the accumulated historical and archeological knowledge exhibiting surprising findings, which portray a picture with numerous parts that are different from the known tradition.

The myth of the exodus from Egypt is especially discussed, and the astonishing similarity between ancient Egyptian theology as documented in surviving papyri, and the monotheism of Moses, including the Ten Commandments and the Hebrew ethical codex, which became over the course of history an established cultural asset of the entire Western civilization.

The outcome of this research is presented to the reader in an easy language accompanied by figures to illustrate the given subjects.

PREFACE

It is hoped that the book will stimulate broadened research of the history and the culture of the Hebrew nation to further enlighten this subject, which is of major interest to Western culture in general.

Chapter I

The Origin of the Hebrews

THE HEBREW CULTURE INCLUDING the monotheistic religion, the common beliefs, and the folklore of the nation cannot be fully understood without studying the historical background of the development and formation of the Jewish nation, whence it came from, and the origin of its culture and religion.

The Mesopotamian heritage—Ur Kasdim

Reading the book of Genesis, chapters 1-19, it is quite impossible to ignore the great similarity between the tales given there and those of the Mesopotamian mythology that has been preserved. The story of the creation of humans from the clay of the earth, abundant in Mesopotamian alluvial soil, is as narrated in the ancient Sumerian poem:

> Come near thou Goddess [Inanna], for sacred is the scene,
> The fertilization rite which repeats for generations,
> For that it is since Enlil (the chief God) created man from naught,
> For that it is since Enlil created man from the clay of earth.[1]

---

1. Ganan, *Sumerian Poems*.

The superiority of God over the mythical powers, the monsters, Yam (יָם—Sea), and Tanin (תַּנִּין—a sea monster) prevailed in the Mesopotamian culture. It is particularly specified: "And God created the great sea-monsters..." (Gen 1, 21).

The mythical powers that undermined God's absolute rule are mentioned again in the biblical text testifying for being well-rooted in the Hebrew mythos. "Awake, awake, put on strength, O arm of the LORD ... *Art thou not it that hewed Rahab in pieces, that pierced Tanin?*" (Isa 51, 9).

And Job asked whether he is a foe or enemy rival to God: "Am I a Sea (יָם—Yam), or Tanin, that Thou settest a watch over me?" (Job 7, 12).

And the might of God against the rival powers "Thou didst break the Sea (יָם—Yam), in pieces by Thy strength; Thou didst shatter the heads of Tanins in the waters", (Ps 74, 13) and "In that day the LORD with His sore and great and strong sword will punish leviathan the slant serpent, and leviathan the tortuous serpent; and He will slay the dragon (תַּנִּין—Tanin in Hebrew) that is in the sea" (Isa 27, 1).

The Slant serpent is a Mesopotamian secondary god that is represented in the star constellation as it appears from the prayer of the ancient priest: "The great gods of night ..., Orion, Slant-serpent".[2]

Interestingly, the serpent as an opposing power to the creating God appears also in the ancient Egyptian myth. In the papyrus of Ani (British Museum), in his exaltation of the supreme god Ra/Re, "Your serpent-foe has been given over to the fire and the rebel-serpent is fallen, his arms are bound, Re has taken away his movements, and as for the sons of impotent revolt, they have no being".[3]

The conflict between the farmer and the shepherd in the early days of human settlement as found in the Mesopotamic

---

2. Klein and Shifra, *In Those Distant Days*; Cassuto, *Ha'ela Anat*.
3. Wallis Budge, *Egyptian Ideas of the Afterlife*.

literature, is again illustrated here by the story of Cain and Abel: "And Abel was a keeper of sheep, but Cain was a tiller of the ground... And it came to pass, when they were in the field, that Cain rose up against Abel his brother, and slew him" (Gen 4, 2-8).

From those days the Hebrew term "גַּן" was preserved; "Gan" (גַּן—garden), and "גַּנָּן" (gardener), the man who guards the planted garden, usually from the invasion of shepherds, (וְגַנּוֹתִי עַל-הָעִיר הַזֹּאת, לְהוֹשִׁיעָהּ," (ישעיהו לז, לה"

"For I will guard this city to save it" (Isa 37, 35).

The Hebrew story of the flood bears much similarity to the Mesopotamian myth. The Hebrew writer meticulously narrated not only the story of building the ark but other details including the sending of the raven and the dove (who came back with the olive leaf—indicating the water was abated; since then, the dove has become the symbol of peace). These details in the Biblical story are specified in the Epic of Gilgamesh, the ancient Mesopotamian, Sumerian king and hero, regarding Utnapishtim, the survivor of the mythological flood "I sent out the Dove (lines 145), I sent out the raven (line 150) (terracotta tablet, Figure I.1).

The Origin of the Hebrews and Their Faith

Figure I.1: Epic of Gilgamesh – story of the flood.

The origin of the Patriarchs

It is clearly inferred from the scripture itself that the ethnic origin of the Patriarchs, the forefathers of the twelve tribes of Israel, is Aram (Haran), northern Syria. This testimony is repeated multiple times from the story of Terah in Genesis up to Joshua.

> *And Abram took Sarai his wife, and Lot his brother's son, and all their substance that they had gathered, and the souls that they had gotten in Haran; and they went forth to go into the land of Canaan (Gen 12, 5).*

> *And: And thou shalt speak and say before the LORD thy God: 'A wandering Aramean (from the country of Aram) was my father, and he went down into Egypt, and sojourned there, few in number; and he became*

there a nation, great, mighty, and populous' (Deut 26, 5).

The mention of the descent of the forefathers from Haran (northern Syria, not Ur-Kasdim) appears again in the book of Joshua: "And Joshua said unto all the people: 'Thus saith the LORD, the God of Israel: Your fathers dwelt of old time beyond the River, even Terah, the father of Abraham, and the father of Nahor; and they served other gods'" (Josh 24, 2).

Beyond the River refers to the great Euphrates River in the north as it is commonly named; thus from the Aram region, consistent with the text in the book of Genesis. It is of note that the preservation of the genetic-family ties is highly emphasized in the book of Genesis.

> And Abraham said unto his servant . . . I will make thee swear by the LORD, the God of heaven and the God of the earth, that thou shalt not take a wife for my son of the daughters of the Canaanites, among whom I dwell. But thou shalt go unto my country, and to my kindred, and take a wife for my son, even for Isaac (Gen 24, 2-4).

There is no "my country" and "my kindred" but Aram. Thus, indeed Rebeca the Aramean woman is married to Abraham's son Isaac. The most prominent example of these ties with Aram is undoubtedly that of the twelve tribes of Israel who are related to Jacob and to his four Aramean women (Leah, Rachel, Bilhah, and Zilpah).

There are numerous external indications that support this ethnic origin. For example, it is particularly prominent in the individuals' names found in texts from the early Bronze Age (about third millennium BCE) in Aram, Ugarit, and Ebla in the north. Names such as Abram, Jacob, and Israel (i.e., God who is the victor; see more below); Israel also appears as an individual's name in scripts from those places.[4]

---

4. Amir, *Gods and Heroes*; Bahat, "Excavations at Tel Mardich"; Bramet and Weizmann, *Elba*; Isserlin, *The Israelites*; Kempinski, "Tel Mardikh-Ebla";

The Origin of the Hebrews and Their Faith

The ethnic tie with Mesopotamia is quite weak and it is mentioned in the Bible only once: "And Terah took Abram his son, and Lot the son of Haran, his son's son, and Sarai his daughter-in-law, his son Abram's wife; and they went forth with them from Ur of the Chaldees, to go into the land of Canaan; and they came unto Haran, and dwelt there" (Gen 11, 31).

In contrast to that weak ethnic relation, the cultural influence of Mesopotamia is notable. This is undoubtedly as a consequence of the strong influence of the Sumerian and Akkadian cultures over the entire Near East. This influence is particularly emphasized by the adoption of the writing system, which then was transformed by the Phoenicians to the phonetic Alef-Bet (A, B; abjad writing system used in Hebrew) known in these days. Consequently, the exposure to the well-developed literature echoed in the stories of Genesis including the story of creation, of the flood (including the mentioning of the raven and the dove, as noted above), the conflict between the farmer and the shepherd, were well adopted. Even the story of Job (why bad things happen to good people) was found on seven clay tablets in the Assyrian royal archive in the capital Nineveh (although the Hebrew philosophical dialogue is different). These documents were preserved by the scholar scribers and they served as the basis for the stories of Genesis in their Hebrew version to emphasize the superiority of God over the mythical opposing powers, such as Yam (Sea) and Tanin. The exile to Babylon probably contributed much to this literal exposure.

It is noteworthy that many names that appear in relationship with the Patriarchs are of Mesopotamian origin; from there they transferred to Aram and from Aram to the land of Canaan. Names of Mesopotamian gods were transformed

---

Kutscher, "Ebla Documents", "Corrections and Additions"; Rin, *The Plots of the Gods*; Tubb, *Canaanites*.

into Hebrew form, like the chief Babylonian god Marduk (Marduch) to Mordechai the Jew, a main personality in the Book of Esther; Issascur is *Yissachar* (son of Jacob, one of the twelve tribes); Isharu became Asher (another son of Jacob, one of the twelve tribes); Isaralim is probably Israel (Arabic إسرائيل Israil); and other names for Gods. Shamaimu is "Shamaim" [Hebrew: שָׁמַיִם—heaven], Dumuzu or Dumuzi is Tammuz (the name of the tenth month in the Hebrew calendar). Dumuzi is the god that represents the changes of the agricultural seasons—dies in the summer—the dry season in the Near East region, and revives in the winter—the season of rain. Interestingly, Tammuz is mentioned in the book of Ezekiel as a subject of worship by the people in the First Temple era:

"Then He brought me to the door of the gate of the LORD'S house which was toward the north; and, behold, there sat the women weeping for Tammuz" (Ezek 8, 14). This is in full accord with the widespread ritual mourning the dead Tammuz in the ancient Near East region as appears in a Sumerian tablet from Nippur (Ni 4486): "She can make the lament for you, my Dumuzid, the lament for you, the lament, the lamentation reach the desert...", "O Dumuzid... she sobs tearfully, lad, husband, lord, sweet as the date...O Dumuzid, she sobs, she sobs tearfully".[5]

Also, Mot [Hebrew: מָוֶת *Maweth*, Arabic موت *mawt*] the god of death, in the Ugaritic myth the brother of the chief god Baal is mentioned in the Bible, "For death (*Maweth*) is come up into our windows, it is entered into our palaces, to cut off the children from the street, and the young men from the broad places" (Jer 9, 20); and "Destruction (*Abadon*) and Death (*Maweth*) said: 'We have heard a rumor thereof with our ears.'" (Job 28, 22).[6]

The term "Elilim" [Hebrew: אֱלִילִים], idols, frequently mentioned in the Bible, is a transformation of the name Enlil,

---

5. Black, Cunningham, Robson, and Zólyomi, *Inana and Bilulu*.
6. Black and Green, *Gods, Demons and Symbols*; Cassuto, *Ha'ela Anat*.

the Sumerian chief deity. The consonant "N" is dropped in the Hebrew language as for example in the Aramaic word Ant (אַנְתְּ, you), which became At (אַתְּ) in Hebrew, or from the Arabic word Anta [أنتَ, you] that became Ata [אַתָּה] in Hebrew.

It is evident, therefore, from these and many other examples, that a major anthology of the ancient deities from Mesopotamia, Ur-Chaldea [Hebrew: אוּר כַּשְׂדִים Ūr Kaśdîm], is well-presented in the Hebrew tradition and faith.

Of special interest is the ancient dramatic story of the Patriarch Abraham, his wife Sarah, her Egyptian bondwoman Hagar, and Ishmael the son of Hagar. Briefly, Abraham had a son, Ishmael, from Sarah's bondwoman Hagar. After Isaac was born to Sarah she insisted on the expulsion of Ishmael and Hagar so as not to let him inherit with Isaac, an act that Abraham disliked. It is interesting to realize that the names involved in this drama are most probably symbolically structured according to their part played in it. *Ab*raham— "and thou shalt be the father of a multitude of nations" (Gen 17, 4) [Hebrew: *Ab* (אָב)—Father]; thus Abraham is the father of nations; Sarah [Hebrew: שָׂרָה; "Sar"—שַׂר] is a chief (in Akkadian—a king or ruler). Thus, Sarah is the chief in her house and could order the expulsion of her Egyptian bondwoman Hagar with her son (born to Abraham), concordant with the script "And God said unto Abraham . . . in all that Sarah saith unto thee, hearken unto her voice . . ." (Gen 21, 12). Hagar is the one who is condemned to expulsion or emigration [Hebrew: Hagar—הָגָר; Arabic: هاجر Hājar, the one who emigrates, Hagira emigration, Le-hager להגר—to emigrate]. It is also noteworthy that the Semitic name Hagar is inconsistent with her said Egyptian origin. And finally, Ishmael is the one that the God hearkened to [Hebrew: יִשְׁמָעֵאל—God will hearken; יִשְׁמַע—Yshma— will hear, אֵל—El—God], as indicated in the Biblical line:

"וַיִּשְׁמַע אֱלֹהִים אֶת קוֹל הַנַּעַר", and God hearkened to the voice of the lad (Gen 21, 17).

As regards the tradition concerning Abraham, it is of interest and maybe with a bit of surprise to realize from the text itself who is the person that left Mesopotamia, Ur-Chaldea, to go to the land of Canaan. "And Terah took Abram his son, and Lot the son of Haran, his son's son, and Sarai his daughter-in-law, his son Abram's wife; and they went forth with them from Ur of the Chaldees to go into the land of Canaan; and they came unto Haran and dwelt there" (Gen 11, 31). Thus, not Abraham, as the tradition holds, but his father Terah is the one who made the move from Ur—Mesopotamia—to the land of Canaan.

The settlement of the Patriarchs in Canaan

The settlement of the Hebrew forefathers in the land of Canaan was associated with significant struggle, and it seems that the land was not endowed to them on a silver-platter by the Devin promise only. The portrayed characters are different from, sometimes even far from, the image held by the tradition. Abraham fights against several kings (rulers of Polis) and defeats them (Gen 14, 14-16). The Philistine Abimelech king of Gerar is careful not to have a conflict with him, and after evaluating the situation he elected to give up, avoiding a struggle with Abraham (Gen 21, 14-15).

Melchizedek king of Salem (the future Jerusalem, "the house of Salem" the Canaanite god) came to meet Abraham and bless him, and the king of Sodom came to ask to receive his men who were set free by the forces organized by Abraham (Gen 14, 18-21). Forces that could defeat the kings that the former coalition against them, including kings of Sodom and Gomorrah, had failed to do so.

The story of Jacob, the person who is described in the scripture as "and Jacob was a quiet man, dwelling in tents" (Gen 25, 27) is full of wars and conflicts.

The Origin of the Hebrews and Their Faith

The conflict of Jacob with Esau is portrayed on a mythical basis for Jacob taking with guile the blessing of Esau from their father Isaac. As a consequence, he had to flee to Haran for fear of his brother Esau. However, in another place the text portrays a cause that seems more realistic:

> And Esau took his wives, and his sons, and his daughters, and all the souls of his house, and his cattle, and all his beasts, and all his possessions, which he had gathered in the land of Canaan; and went into a land away from his brother Jacob ... And Esau dwelt in the mountain-land of Seir—Esau is Edom (Gen 36, 6-8).

Thus, not Jacob who traditionally is seen as a weak, quiet man is running from the fighter Esau, but Esau had to desert the battle field, vacating the area for the stronger force.

Also, the conflict with Esau after Jacob crossed the Jabbok River (Gen 32, 23) ended with the Edomite force of Esau returning to their place while Jacob continues his journey to Canaan as planned. The struggle in the Jabbok ford is portrayed many years later in the nation's folklore as a mystical wrestle: "And Jacob was left alone; and there wrestled a man with him until the breaking of the day" (Gen 32, 25). However, the Jabbok River is the border between the Gilead Mountains in the north and the mountains of Edom in the south. On both its banks there is a wide fertile valley, the valley of Sukkot. Thus, crossing the Jabbok may present a threat to the local populations, a reason why would Esau with his men rushed to the site after Jacob and his men crossed the stream.

The strength of Jacob in that chapter is emphasized again by the script; before the crossing there was a struggle, where Jacob was hurt but emerged as a victor: "And he said: 'Thy name shall be called no more Jacob, but Israel; for thou hast striven with God and with men, and hast prevailed'" (Gen 32, 29) and Jacob continues on his way to settle in the land of Canaan. (*Yisra⊠el*, "struggle with God", i.e., a man capable of struggling with God).

The conflict with Laban the Aramaean, the brother of Jacob's mother Rebecca, is presented again as a family quarrel:

> And Laban said to Jacob: 'What hast thou done, that thou hast outwitted me, and carried away my daughters as though captives of the sword? Wherefore didst thou flee secretly, and outwit me; and didst not tell me, that I might have sent thee away with mirth and with songs, with tabret and with harp; and didst not suffer me to kiss my sons and my daughters? now hast thou done foolishly' (Gen 31, 26-28).

Then, had that been the case, why did they have to make a covenant and set a border between them?

> And Laban answered and said unto Jacob: ... And now come, let us make a covenant, I and thou; and let it be for a witness between me and thee ... And Jacob said unto his brethren: 'Gather stones'; and they took stones, and made a heap. And they did eat there by the heap. And Laban called it Jegar-sahadutha; but Jacob called it Galeed ... And Laban said to Jacob: 'Behold this heap, and behold the pillar, which I have set up betwixt me and thee. This heap be witness, and the pillar be witness, that I will not pass over this heap to thee, and that thou shalt not pass over this heap and this pillar unto me, for harm ... And Jacob swore by the God of his father Isaac' (Gen 31, 43-53).

It is truly surprising that the strong man Laban, as he is portrayed, is the one who is afraid of Jacob, asking that he not cross the border to his land. By doing so he is cutting off all his ties with his dear daughters and grandchildren, forever. Thus, a family issue may not be the underlying reason for him pursuing Jacob, an act that apparently ended in avoiding a clash. And what is the indication of the sentence "and Jacob said unto his brethren", mentioned there? It seems that Jacob was not alone.

The story of the war between the children of Jacob (to become the twelve tribes) and the inhabitants of Shechem is again portrayed in a narrative-mythical way, as avenging their sister Dinah's rape by the son of the Shechem ruler (although the kidnaper desired to marry her as a lawful wife; Gen 34). According to the scripture, the attack resulted in the destruction of all males of the city (Gen 34, 25). It is clear, however, that fighting and conquering such a central city as Shechem requires a strong warrior force. These struggles must be central in the conquest of the land of Canaan, as is confirmed elsewhere by Jacob himself (Gen 48, 24). See also Chapter III with the complaint of the ruler of Shechem against attackers (the term Hapiru or Apiru mentioned there as a group of nomad-warriors). However, the association of it with the term Hebrews is highly controversial, primarily because it is not related to a specific ethnic group, and Hapiru are also mentioned in other regions of the Near East.

In regard to the settlement of the twelve tribes in the Land of Canaan, the conflict between Joseph and his brother is depicted in the Book of Genesis as a personal one, maybe to lessen its impact. However, the statement of Jacob by the end of his days is highly significant. Jacob is granting the right for land to the two descendants of his son Joseph, a right for a land equal to that of his other sons, the tribes of Israel: "And now thy two sons . . ., Ephraim and Manasseh, even as Reuben and Simeon, shall be mine" (Gen 48, 5).

It seems that the writer failed to realize that he already placed Ephraim the younger before Manasseh the older, this is before Jacob himself granted this priority of first-born to Ephraim. "And Israel stretched out his right hand, and laid it upon Ephraim's head, who was the younger, and his left hand upon Manasseh's head, guiding his hands wittingly;

for Manasseh was the first-born" (Gen 48, 14). And Jacob is making a prediction:

> And Joseph said unto his father: 'Not so, my father, for this is the first-born; put thy right hand upon his head.' And his father refused, and said: 'I know it, my son, I know it; he also shall become a people, and he also shall be great; howbeit his younger brother shall be greater than he, and his seed shall become a multitude of nations' (Gen 48, 18-19).

And indeed, according to Jacob's prophecy, the tribe of Ephraim was the larger and the dominant one. Thus, it seems that this narration regarding the position of Ephraim reflects the actual situation at the time of writing that text. This reality is supported by the ancient narrative (related to Moses), "And of Joseph he said: Blessed of the LORD be his land . . . and the good will of Him that dwelt in the bush (God); let the blessing come upon the head of Joseph, and upon the crown of the head of him that is *prince among his brethren*"; and the strength of Ephraim the decedent of Joseph is especially emphasized "and his horns are the horns of the wild-ox; with them he shall gore the peoples all of them . . . and they are the ten-thousands of *Ephraim*, and they are the thousands of *Manasseh*" (Deut 33, 13-17).

It is of special significance that on this very occasion Jacob clearly indicates that the right for land heritage he is giving to the sons of Joseph is for a land that he had conquered in war. "And Israel said unto Joseph: . . . Moreover I have given to thee one portion above thy brethren, which I took out of the hand of the Amorite *with my sword and with my bow*" (Gen 48, 21-22).

History shows that the Amorite was a strong people who occupied a large part of the Near East including Canaan. Therefore, a victory over them necessitates a strong force with significant warring capacity. How these facts conform to the traditional image of Jacob as a pacific man "and

Jacob was a quiet man, dwelling in tents" (Genesis 25, 27) remained unclear.

This chapter in Genesis is of particular interest. It is eventually explaining the rather incomprehensible behavior of the sons of Jacob, that according to the script sold their brother Joseph to slavery out of jealousy: "Now Israel loved Joseph more than all his children, because he was the son of his old age; and he made him a coat of many colours" (Gen 37, 3). The first clue is the double dream of Joseph being a ruler over his brothers "we were binding sheaves in the field, and, lo, my sheaf arose, and also stood upright; and, behold, your sheaves came round about, and bowed down to my sheaf", and "Behold, I have dreamed yet a dream: and, behold, the sun and the moon and eleven stars bowed down to me" (Gen 37, 7-9). Dreams rose in significant opposition around him. The dream is completed by the outcome (though it is told as having happened in the land of Egypt), the power of Joseph is increased and from him emerged two separate tribes, Ephraim and Manasseh, with right for a land equal to that of the eleven brethren, the children of Jacob. Therefore, it seems that the story of granting this right for land by Jacob himself was written *post factum* with the intent to provide legitimization to this exceptional right given only to the descendants of Joseph. One of these two tribes, the tribe of Ephraim, is demanding hegemony over all the other tribes of Israel.[7]

When (in highly lyrical language) the prophet Jerimiah mourns the destruction of Samaria, the capital of the kingdom of Israel, the name of the kingdom is not mentioned but that of Ephraim: "Is Ephraim (not) a darling son unto Me? Is he (not) a child that is dandled? For as often as I speak of

---

7. According to the scripture, Jacob had 11 sons who, with the two descendants of his son Joseph, formed the twelve tribes of the nation of Israel. Later on in history, they became two kingdoms, the kingdom of Judah with the tribes of Judah and Benjamin, and the kingdom of Israel with rest of the ten tribes.

him, I do earnestly remember him still; therefore My heart yearneth for him, I will surely have compassion upon him, saith the LORD" (Jer 31, 19). Furthermore, in the consolation prophesy for the return of the scattered people of Israel, the prophet Isaiah mentions Ephraim: "And it shall come to pass in that day, that the Lord will set His hand again the second time to recover the remnant of His people", then "The envy also of Ephraim shall depart, and they that harass Judah shall be cut off; Ephraim shall not envy Judah, and Judah shall not vex Ephraim" (Isa 11, 11, 13). Thus, Ephraim is the dominant one of the ten tribes, and he is the one who represents the kingdom of Israel.

The Matriarchs and the twelve tribes of Israel

It has already been mentioned that according to the scripture and to the well-rooted tradition among Jewish people, all the Nation of Israel is the descendant of one ancestor, Jacob, and his four women who begot the eleven children to become the twelve tribes of Israel (Joseph establishing the two tribes, Ephraim and Manasseh).

This tradition became an essential fact in the formation of the nation of Israel. It is repeatedly mentioned across all the books of Bible, and along the history of the Jewish people. In general, it seems that the ancient writer made in this section a work intended to establish this as a fact, most probably based on a prevalent mythical belief that was conceived as a vital ideology required to support the integration of the separate tribes into one nation. This dogma seems central to the practical need of the assimilation, which was essential for the ability to form power sufficient to occupy the land of Canaan from its inhabitants.

Reading the event of Jacob sojourning with his uncle Laban (brother of Rebecca his mother) in Haran (a northern region), reveals an extensive dealing with the relationships between the mothers Leah and Rachel and the involvement of their maidservants Bilhah and Zilpah with a specific indication of the birth of each child (the future tribes of Israel). In a superficial consideration, the story may be seen as common human-social affairs, in those days and today. However, looking more carefully into the details reveals a surprising phenomenon that can be explained in the given circumstances only on the ideological background of the common origin of the nation, as being related to one ancestor.

In this section, citing the original text from Genesis 29 to 30 is becoming difficult. This is primarily due to the Hebrew terms and language being used there, which are highly sophisticated involving vocal synonyms, language rhythm, idiomatic phrases, and metaphors at a poetic level that even Hebrew-language speakers would have difficulty to fully comprehend. Thus, translation into another language will inevitably cause missing these fine nuances of the Hebrew language used in these chapters. This language is particularly employed in naming the children, providing an underlying reason for the given names; this by using a highly poetic language, their practical significance is given later.

Hence is a summary of the text from Genesis 29 to 30.

> *And Leah conceived, and bore a son, and she called his name Reuben; for she said: 'Because the LORD hath looked upon my affliction; for now my husband will love me.'* [Hebrew: רְאוּבֵן Reuben—literally: see a male child, רְאוּ—Reuh—see, בֵּן—Ben, male child] *And she conceived again, and bore a son; and said: 'Because the LORD hath heard that I am hated, He hath therefore given me this son also.' And she called his name Simeon* [Hebrew: שִׁמְעוֹן—Shimon, for God שָׁמַע Shama—heard].

And she conceived again, and bore a son; and said: 'Now this time will my husband be joined unto me, because I have borne him three sons.' Therefore was his name called Levi [Hebrew: לֵוִי—Levi, for this time my husband יִלָּוֶה—Yilaveh—join].

And she conceived again, and bore a son; and she said: 'This time will I praise the LORD.' Therefore she called his name Judah ...." [Hebrew: Judah is יְהוּדָה—*Yehuda*, and praise or thank the LORD is "אוֹדֶה אֶת-יְהוָֹה"—*Odeh et Adonai*] (Gen 29, 33-35).

And the barren Rachel is following her, and when Bilhah her maidservant had born to Jacob a child "And Rachel said: 'God hath judged me, and hath also heard my voice, and hath given me a son.' Therefore called she his name Dan." (Gen 30, 6) [Hebrew: דָּן—*Dan*, and judged me is דָּנַנִּי—*Dan*ani].

"And Bilhah Rachel's handmaid conceived again, and bore Jacob a second son; And Rachel said: 'With mighty wrestlings have I wrestled with my sister, and have prevailed.' And she called his name Naphtali" [Hebrew: נַפְתָּלִי—*Naphtali*, and wrestlings is נַפְתּוּלֵי—*Naphtuley*] (Gen 30, 6-8).

And Leah followed Rachel's method: "When Leah saw that she had left off bearing, she took Zilpah her handmaid, and gave her to Jacob to wife. And Zilpah Leah's handmaid bore Jacob a son. And Leah said: 'Fortune is come!' And she called his name Gad" [Hebrew: גָּד—Gad is fortune or luck] (Gen 30, 9-11). Then "And Zilpah Leah's handmaid bore Jacob a second son. And Leah said: 'Happy am I! for the daughters will call me happy.' And she called his name Asher" (Gen 30, 12-13) [Hebrew: אָשֵׁר—*Asher*, and בְּאָשְׁרִי—B*eoshri*—in my happiness].

And the rush of birth has not ceased yet and the mothers continue their way.

> And Leah said: 'God hath given me my hire, because I gave my handmaid to my husband. And she called his name Issachar" (Gen 30, 18) [Hebrew: יִשָּׂשכָר—Issachar, and שְׂכָרִי—*Sechari*—my reward]. And Leah conceived again, and bore a sixth son to Jacob. And Leah said: 'God hath endowed me with a good dowry; now will my husband dwell with me, because I have borne him six sons.' And she called his name Zebulun (Gen 30, 19-20) [Hebrew:—זְבֻלוּן—Zebulun,

and יְזְבְּלֵנִי—Izbeleni, and זְבָדַנִי—Zebadani endowed me with a good dowry].

Now Rachel herself is joining the contest and she is giving birth "And God remembered Rachel, and God hearkened to her, and opened her womb. And she conceived, and bore a son, and said: 'God hath taken away my reproach.' And she called his name Joseph, saying: "The LORD will add to me another son" (Gen 30, 22-24) [Hebrew: יוֹסֵף—Yosef—Joseph, and יֹסֵף יְהֹוָה לִי, בֵּן אַחֵר—LORD will add (Yosef) to me another son].

And here to the patient reader who follows the events of Jacob's sojourning with Laban (his uncle, the father of Leah and Rachel), awaits an interesting puzzle. After the escape of Jacob from Laban as described previously, and the chase of Laban, which ended peacefully, to the luck of the future Jewish nation, here is a summary:

> And Laban answered and said unto Jacob: And now come, let us make a covenant, I and thou; and let it be for a witness between me and thee ... And Jacob said unto his brethren: 'Gather stones'; and they took stones, and made a heap. And they did eat there by the heap. And Laban called it Jegar-sahadutha; but Jacob called it Galeed (Gen 31, 43-53).

It seems that Laban the Aramite was not familiar with the Hebrew language of Jacob, which called the covenant hip of stones גַּלְעֵד—Gal'ed, literally: Gal is a heap, and Ed is a witness, consistent with the words "let it be for a witness", but Laban called it "יְגַר שָׂהֲדוּתָא" Jegar-sahadutha, which is the exact translation in the Aramaic language.

Now comes the inevitable question: how is that conceivable that the Aramean daughters of Laban himself, who were most probably illiterate (being shepherdesses), not even knowing the spelling of a word in the Aramaic language itself, as the custom of these days (about 1500 BCE), exhibit an admirable knowledge in the Hebrew language that even

The Origin of the Hebrews

scholars of the language would have difficulty to reach. The phrases given in naming the children, as mentioned above, employ a highly sophisticated language as only a highly Hebrew-literate person could appreciate. Phrases which necessitate high education, well-developed poetic skills, and proficiency in the Hebrew language itself.

A good reason for the particular dealing with the names of the tribes may well be to emphasize their Hebrew ethnicity, as names that are rooted in the Hebrew language, rather than being of Aramaic or Mesopotamian origin. As mentioned, many of these names are actually found in the northern regions (Syria) such as Ugarit and Ebla. Thus, the author here made extensive effort to base these names on Hebrew terms, primarily by using phonetic synonyms. This was remarkably done also with the name Israel יִשְׂרָאֵל—*Yisra*❒*el*, which was prevalent in the region and is found until nowadays among the remnant of the Assyrian people, called Chaldeans (many are living now in the United States). Here, in order to sanctify the name as is given by God, specifically to the father of the Hebrew nation Jacob, appeared the following sentence "And he said: 'Thy name shall be called no more Jacob, but Israel; for thou hast striven with God and with men, and hast prevailed'" (Gen 32, 29). The author is exhibiting again his mastery of the language to give a special Hebrew meaning to a name known in the region, i.e., "striven with God": Israel יִשְׂרָאֵל: *Yisra*❒*el*, Ysra-El, Ysra-prevail/rule, El-god, i.e., a man who could strive with god, whereas the direct meaning is "God prevail" or "God rule".

"בִּשְׁנַת שָׁלוֹשׁ, לְמָלְכוֹ, עָשָׂה מִשְׁתֶּה, לְכָל-שָׂרָיו וַעֲבָדָיו: חֵיל פָּרַס וּמָדַי, הַפַּרְתְּמִים וְשָׂרֵי הַמְּדִינוֹת—לְפָנָיו". , "In the third year of his reign, he (King Achashverosh) made a feast unto all his princes [שָׂרָיו] and his servants; the army of Persia and Media, the nobles and princes [שָׂרֵי] of the provinces, being before him." (Esth 1, 3) שַׂר—Sar ruler or prince in Akkadian].

In order to give a special Hebrew meaning to the name Israel attributed to Jacob, the author here is using a verb derived from the adjective Sar, i.e., "Ysra", the one who exercises the role of Sar, i.e., ruling. This verb was used later by Isaiah[8] as shown above, as an adjective [שָׂרִים—Sarim princes, and יָשֹׂרוּ—Yasoru, rule], and El is God [from Akkadian Ilu-god, any major god in the region; El is a singular, later becoming plural Elohim—אֱלֹהִים in Hebrew]. Thus, Ysrael denotes "God Rule" or "God will rule". In that sentence of justification for giving Jacob the name Israel, the English translation of שָׂרִיתָ is "hast striven (with God and with men)". Thus, the author is providing it with a special meaning expressed by the phrase "hast successfully striven" here with God and with men, endowing Jacob the father of the tribes with a high-ranked title.

In conclusion, it seems quite inevitable to arrive at the conclusion that this chapter was written with the intent to further strengthen and establish the ideological concept of the unified origin of the tribes from one family and a single ancestor bearing the name Israel. This mythos was most probably necessary to reinforce the consolidation of the various tribes who lived in the region into a single, cohesive society with sufficiently collaborative power capable of conquering the land and forming a state (more on this in Chapter III).

It is noteworthy that this idea of family unity is prevalent throughout the entire narrative of the Torah (*Pentateuch*—the first five books of the Bible) and the following books, from the story of the Patriarchs up to the formation of the kingdom. A unity that was needed to battle the forces of the other ethnic groups in the region, including the strong one of the "Sea people", the Philistines.

However, despite the attempt to portray the early Hebrews as a unique ethnic group with specific origin, language, and culture, the script itself largely testifies against this assumption, certainly at that time in history. The twelve

---

8. "הֵן לְצֶדֶק, יִמְלָךְ-מֶלֶךְ; וּלְשָׂרִים, לְמִשְׁפָּט יָשֹׂרוּ", "Behold, a king shall reign in righteousness, and as for princes, they shall rule in justice" (Isa 32, 1).

tribes lived among a mixed multitude of Canaanite tribes in the region, having common culture and speaking the same language. The names, for example, of the Edomite family look like pure Hebrew names, some being used until today (marked in Bold):

> *These are the names of Esau's sons:* **Eliphaz** *the son of* **Adah** *the wife of Esau, Reuel the son of* **Basemath** *the wife of Esau. And the sons of Eliphaz were Teman, Omar, Zepho, and Gatam, and* **Kenaz** *(Atniel son of Kenaz, the first Judge after the death of Joshua) . . . And these are the sons of Reuel: Nahath, and* **Zerah**, **Shammah** *. . . And . . .* **Oholibamah** *. . . and she bore to Esau Jeush, and Jalam, and* **Korah** *[a famous Priest—Cohanim family served in the temple of Solomon] . . . and his wife's name was Mehetabel, the daughter of Matred, the daughter of* **Mei-Zahab** *(Gen 36, 10), [Hebrew:* מֵי זָהָב*—Mei-Zahab is Gold-Water; after more than three thousand years, the name is still found among Jewish people, in its German form as GoldWasser].*

It is important to note that through all the books of the Bible there is numerous evidence that the Hebrews had common culture and were worshipping common idols with the people of the region. The Hebrews never ceased worshipping major regional idols such as Baal, Ashera (Astrat)—the fertility goddess, Chemosh—god of Moabites, and all the pantheon of gods of the Semitic nations in the region.

A testimony is from the reform in favor of the faith in יְהֹוָה—YHWH [Hebrew pronounced Adonai—Lord] by King Josiah—יֹאשִׁיָּהוּ.

> *And the king commanded Hilkiah the high priest . . . to bring forth out of the temple of the LORD all the vessels that were made for Baal, and for the Asherah, and for all the host of heaven; and he burned them without Jerusalem . . . And he put down the idolatrous priests, whom the kings of Judah had ordained to offer in the high places in the cities of Judah, and*

> *in the places round about Jerusalem; them also that offered unto Baal, to the sun, and to the moon, and to the constellations, and to all the host of heaven . . .*
>
> *And he brought out the Asherah from the house of the LORD, without Jerusalem, and burned it at the brook Kidron . . . And he broke down the houses of the sodomites, that were in the house of the LORD, where the women wove coverings for the Asherah (2 Kgs, 23, 4-7).*

Of interest is the unique finding of an inscription from the early days of the kingdom (the ninth century BCE) found in Khirbat Al-Kum near Hebron, bearing a blessing by the name of יְהוָה—YHWH—Adonai, and his consort Ashera—אֲשֵׁרָה (see Figure V.1).

The fact that this Idolatry was highly prevalent and so embedded within the culture of the Hebrews is also evidenced from the testimony of the people themselves.

After the destruction of Jerusalem by the Babylonians, 587 BCE, which is presented as a punishment by God, the remnant Jews (i.e., citizens of Judah) still refused to worship יְהוָה—YHWH. Said the prophet Jeremiah to the remnant of the people:

> *Thus saith the LORD of hosts, the God of Israel: Ye have seen all the evil that I have brought upon Jerusalem, and upon all the cities of Judah; and, behold, this day they are a desolation, and no man dwelleth therein; because of their wickedness which they have committed to provoke Me, in that they went to offer, and to serve other gods, whom they knew not, neither they, nor ye, nor your fathers. Howbeit I sent unto you all My servants the prophets, sending them betimes and often, saying: Oh, do not this abominable thing that I hate. But they hearkened not, nor inclined their ear to turn from their wickedness, to forbear offering unto other gods. Wherefore My fury and Mine anger was poured forth, and was kindled in the cities of Judah and in the streets of Jerusalem; and they are wasted and desolate, as at this day (Jer 44, 2-6).*

The Origin of the Hebrews

And remarkable is the answer of the remnant of the people and its justification:

> *Then all the men ... and all the women that stood by, a great assembly ... answered Jeremiah, saying:*
>
> *As for the word that thou hast spoken unto us in the name of the LORD, we will not hearken unto thee ... But we will certainly perform every word that is gone forth out of our mouth, to offer unto the queen of heaven, and to pour out drink-offerings unto her, as we have done, we and our fathers, our kings and our princes, in the cities of Judah, and in the streets of Jerusalem; for then had we plenty of food, and were well, and saw no evil. But since we let off to offer to the queen of heaven, and to pour out drink-offerings unto her, we have wanted all things, and have been consumed by the sword and by the famine (Jer 44, 15-19).*

This testimony is well supported by archeological findings that the image of the fertility goddess Asterat [Hebrew: אֲשֵׁרָה—Ashera], which was worshipped throughout the Near East, was found in large numbers in Jerusalem of that time.[9]

---

9. Tubb, *Canaanites*, Figure V.2.

Chapter II

Exodus—Myth and Reality

The myth of Exodus

ONE OF THE MOST prevalent subjects in the literature dealing with the origin of the Hebrews and their foundation is the story of Exodus [Greek: ἔξοδος, *éxodos*—going out], the emergence of the Hebrew people from long-lasting slavery in Egypt. No wonder that this became a major subject of discussion in history and theology for its special significance. In Exodus the emerging people were crystalized to become the Hebrew nation. They were organized into a national society, adapted a new faith, the abstract monotheism of God YHWH [יְהוָה], and settled in the chosen land, the land of Canaan; later to become the Holy Land, the Land of Israel, where their history and culture are strongly bound. A culture developed by a small nation, which would have a crucial influence on the theology and the moral-social values of the entire Western civilization.

The most surprising point in the research of Exodus is the entire lack of any historical reference (except the Hebrew Bible) to this central event, and there is no archeological document or clue that can testify to the existence of that event. It's even more surprising, knowing that in those days Egypt had been a well-organized empire for at least two thousand years. Documentation of such an event was central and common, as for example the conquest of the town of Gezer by Pharaoh Shishak (925 BCE).

> *And it came to pass in the fifth year of king Rehoboam, that Shishak king of Egypt came up against Jerusalem, because they had dealt treacherously with the LORD, with twelve hundred chariots, and threescore thousand horsemen; and the people were without number that came with him out of Egypt; the Lubim, the Sukkiim, and the Ethiopians. And he took the fortified cities which pertained to Judah, and came unto Jerusalem (1 Chr 12:2-4).*

Or the conquest of the city of Kadesh, which is well-documented in the Egyptian writings. A myriad of correspondence has been found between the kings of Egypt and those of Assur, and many others have been found in Al Amarna remains (Amarna letters) between the kings of Egypt and the rulers of the cities of Canaan such as Shechem, but none mention Hebrew, Israel, or Exodus. Egypt was the empire that ruled over that area for a long time.

It is important to note, in relation to the history of the Hebrew faith, that the Book of Torah (the first five books of the Hebrew Bible) was "discovered" many years later. It was in the time of Josiah king of Judah (640-609 BCE), who commanded the restoration of the temple in Jerusalem (2 Kgs 22-23) and who later died in a battle with the Egyptian army. It was during that restoration of the temple when the Chief Priest Hilkiah came with the book, showing it to Shaphan the royal scriber.

> *And Hilkiah the high priest said unto Shaphan the scribe: 'I have found the book of the Law in the house of the LORD.' And Hilkiah delivered the book to*

> *Shaphan, and he read it ... And Shaphan the scribe told the king, saying: 'Hilkiah the priest hath delivered me a book.' And Shaphan read it before the king. And it came to pass, when the king had heard the words of the book of the Law, that he rent his clothes. And the king commanded Hilkiah the priest, and Ahikam the son of Shaphan, and Achbor the son of Micaiah, and Shaphan the scribe, and Asaiah the king's servant, saying: 'Go ye, inquire of the LORD for me, and for the people, and for all Judah, concerning the words of this book that is found; for great is the wrath of the LORD that is kindled against us, because our fathers have not hearkened unto the words of this book, to do according unto all that which is written concerning us (2 Kgs 22:8–13).*

It is clear from the testimony of the scholars (the scribes), the royal officials, and the king himself that this book was not known to them until that time. Thus, it is conceivable that what is written concerning the story of Exodus as we know it was done hundreds of years after the presumed event, based on the mythological tales embedded in the collective memory of the nation and may be remnants of written old texts.

When considering the possibility of the existence of the event of sojourning for a long time (more than 400 years according to the scripture), and the emergence from there, it is prudent to estimate the inevitable consequences of such a stay and events. First of all, the influence of the highly developed Egyptian culture on shepherd people with a much inferior culture as the Canaanites used to live in the Land of Canaan, needs to be considered. The great pyramid already stood there for about 1000 years before the emergence of the Biblical Abraham. What is the magnitude of such an influence after 400 years? Everyone can judge from their own experience of cultural influence for much shorter times on current societies, and infer the high impact of the Egyptians on the Hebrews after such a long period. Though there are many examples, we will refer to the sojourn of the same people in the Babylonian exile after the destruction of the first temple and Jerusalem (586 BCE). In that instance it is well-documented that the exiled people sojourned in Babylon for only 70 years, about 2-3 generations, and even after their return there were still people who remembered the first temple, i.e., a period of only one-sixth that of staying in Egypt. And what were the consequences? Despite already having their well-developed culture, they adopted Babylonian names, where the name of leader of the returning people [שָׁבֵי צִיּוֹן—those who returned to Zion, Jerusalem] is Zeruba-bel (Bel is the chief god of Babylon and its capital city Ba-Bel). The Hebrew names of the months (see Gezer tablet from the first temple area: month Asif (collection of fruits), month of sawing, month of harvest, and so on), had been replaced with names of Babylonian gods including the known god Tamuz (Dumuzu in Mesopotamian languages). Above all, the Hebrew writing itself was replaced by the squared Aramaic writing used in Babylon (important for those who are seeking Torah secrets in the current writing structure). Even the Aramaic language spoken in Babylon became the common language of the people in the Land of Israel.

In contrast to these profound cultural influences after only 70 years, after more than 400 years in Egypt ("And it came to pass at the end of *four hundred and thirty years* ... that all the host of the LORD went out from the land of Egypt" (Exod 12:41)), there is maybe not a single Egyptian word in the Hebrew language, and the names of those who emerged from Egypt are all pure Hebrew. Even the name of Moses [מֹשֶׁה—Mosheh] is Hebrew although it is put in the mouth of daughter of Pharaoh: "And the child grew, and she brought him unto Pharaoh's daughter, and he became her son. And she called his name Moses, and said: 'Because I drew him out of the water.'" כִּי מִן-הַמַּיִם מְשִׁיתִהוּ (Exod 2:10).

Another important indicator is that all the gods of the Canaanite region are well-known and worshiped by the

Hebrews: Baal the chief Canaanite god, Kemosh the god of Moab, Milcom the god of Amon (nowadays Aman), and above all Astrat or Ashtoret [Hebrew עֲשְׁתֹּרֶת; from there came Esther—אֶסְתֵּר] the consort of Baal. Both Baal and Ashtoret were placed in the temple of the Hebrew God YHWH [יְהוָה] many times, as the scripture testifies. "For Solomon went after Ashtoreth the goddess of the Zidonians, and after Milcom the detestation of the Ammonites" (1 Kgs 11:5). Even Mesopotamian gods are well-imbedded in the Hebrew culture; Marduch the Babylonian god became Mordechai the Jew in the book of Esther, and even the ancient Mesopotamian god Tamuz (Dumuzu) who dies and resurrects in the annual seasons, is worshiped in the holy YHWH temple in Jerusalem ("Then ... to the gate of the LORD'S house ... and, behold, there sat the women weeping for Tammuz.") (Ezek 8:14).

However, despite the general term of "gods of Egypt" that is mentioned by the prophets, none of the multitude of Egyptian gods are mentioned in particular, nor it is mentioned they were worshiped by the people.

The entire lack of any traces of the influence of Egyptian culture on the Hebrews, even in time close to the mythological event of Exodus (before the era of Judges, late Bronze Era, around 1550 BCE, where Egypt ruled over the area), inevitably reaches the conclusion that the roots of the Hebrew culture are in the Near East, and neither the origin nor its culture at any time originated in Egypt.

There is even no need to question the inconceivable number of people who emerged from Egypt: "And the children of Israel journeyed from Rameses to Succoth, about *six hundred thousand men on foot, beside children*". (Exod 12:37) Technical arguments are not as important as the essential ones. A wider discussion, based on the research of the history and the supportive archeological findings is given below.

Moses and the Exodus

In considering the creation of the nation of Israel there is a prominent subject integrated into it, a subject that is difficult to find an easy explanation for. This subject is the existence of the man Moses, his relation to the formation of the Hebrew nation on one hand and his relation to the event of Exodus for which no supporting evidence has been found on the other hand. Exodus is the major event in the historiosophy of the Jewish people, the event that led to its formation, from the ethnic crystallization to the spiritual foundation. Here, is the first time that the supreme God is revealing himself in a new name, which was not known to nation's forefathers. The God YHWH—יְהוָה—himself is declaring that this is his name from now on, a name that was not known before (see below, Exod 6:3). This God is connected by the newly formed relations with the evolving society not only by the theological aspect, though this is added later on, but by a functional aspect. "I am the LORD your God, who brought you forth out of the land of Egypt, . . . to be your God" (Lev 25:38). Thus, the functional element and the theological element are interwoven together without the ability to separate them. Later on, God is demonstarting the new theology by imposing a multitude of commands, in part very difficult to follow. However, He is demanding full compliance from his chosen group, and that authority is again justified by the deed of Exodus, the bringing the people out of the land of Egypt.

In the beginning of the Ten Commandments, God is identifying himself for the first time to the people, emphasizing his exclusiveness by the special deed, "I am the LORD thy God, who brought thee out of the land of Egypt, out of the house of bondage. Thou shalt have no other gods before Me" (Exod 20:2). Then, he is warning the people "Thou shalt not bow down unto them, nor serve them; for I the LORD thy God am a jealous God" (Exod 20:5).

The Origin of the Hebrews and Their Faith

The relation between YHWH—יְהוָה—as the God of Israel and the one who brought them out of Egypt is essential for establishing the new faith. It is thus repeated many times in the books of Torah, by the spiritual leaders the prophets, and by dominant leaders such as Joshua. Further, it is presented even many years later as the essence of the faith by the Jewish scholar and philosopher to the pagan king of Cosar (a kingdom that prevailed between the eleventh and seventeenth centuries in part of what is Russia today, at a certain time its king was converted to Judaism). In the book *The Cosar*, written to defend the Jewish faith by Yehudah Halevi (1075—1141), a Jewish scholar, philosopher, poet and physician, the Jewish scholar in his prolog to the Cosar king is declaring the act of Exodus as a major and essential pillar of the Jewish belief. "Said the Scholar, we believe in the God of Abraham, Itshak and Ya'acov [Abraham, Isaac, and Jacob] who brought up the children of Israel from Egypt."

Transforming God into a national god involved the formation of the people themselves as a nation, bringing them up out of Egypt and crystalizing them as a social, ethnic entity. Here is the key to understanding the term "The Chosen People"—these are the people who were chosen by their god: "For thou art a ... people ... LORD thy God hath chosen thee to be His own treasure, out of all peoples that are upon the face of the earth" (Deut 7:6). However, in parallel, this god is also the exclusive one that the people chose, as emphasized in the ancient Hebrew text of the "Song of Deborah", "They (Israel) chose new god" (Judg 5:8). And the mutual covenant is summarized: "And I will ... be your God, and ye shall be My people" (Lev 26:12), and again "Thou hast avouched the LORD this day to be thy God ... And the LORD hath avouched thee this day to be His own people" (Deut 26:17–18).

And, here all these marvelous acts of bringing out the Hebrews from Egypt, crystalizing them into a nation in a long and difficult journey (40 years according to the scripture), creation of the special, unique, and mutual tie between the revealed God and the people in formation, all these tremendous acts are related to a single man, to the man Moses.

Here comes the difficulty. As mentioned, and will be further discussed, the event of Exodus is a very difficult subject to comprehend from a historical point of view. Not only is there no historical support to it and no objective evidence or document for the existence of such a tremendous event, but all existing evidence refutes the proposed way of the creation of the nation of Israel.

However, even if we relate the event of Exodus to an ancient mythology rooted so deeply in the collective conscious of the people, the enigma of the man Moses is still more difficult to resolve. All the extensive theology, from the faith in God, his theological determination "And God said unto Moses: 'I AM THAT I AM'" (Exod 3:14), and his practical naming YHWH—יְהוָה "And God said moreover unto Moses: 'Thus shalt thou say unto the children of Israel: יְהוָה" -The LORD, ... hath sent me unto you; this is My name for ever, and this is My memorial unto all generations" (Exod 3:15) are related to Moses.

Further, all the characteristics of God, the way of his worship with of the formation of the mobile temple, the Tabernacle, his commands and ordinance, his ethical-social laws, and even the definition of the territory of each tribe in the land that God endowed them, all are strongly related to the man Moses. Moses, as the supreme, spiritual, and political authority, according to it the nation will act. Even the authority of Joshua the conqueror of the land of Canaan is directly related to Moses "so did Moses command Joshua; and so did Joshua; he left nothing undone of all that the LORD commanded Moses" (Josh 11:5).

The might of Moses in the consciousness of the people is as of a divine one, "Moses the man of God" (Deut 33:1). The immense status of Moses continues to be built in the Jewish tradition for generations. The Jewish Law Halacha—הֲלָכָה—is justified as commanded by Moses: "הלכה למשה מסיני"—a Law given to Moses in Sinai (the mount of God revelation). And in the indications of the basic principles of the Jewish faith given by Maimonides (רמב״ם, רבנו משה בן מימון) "and Moses is true, his Torah is true".

The spiritual might of Moses is well reflected in the sayings of the Jewish sages in discussing the Torah sentence "And he (Moses) was buried in the valley in the land of Moab over against Beth-peor; *and no man knoweth of his sepulchre unto this day*" (Deut 34:6). They argued that if his burial place was known, they would have made him a deity.

After having evidenced how deeply rooted is the recognition of Moses's high status, we are compelled to go back to the Exodus event and ask the crucial question, how is that possible? If there is no evidence for Exodus, what is now the state of Moses? However, as discussed, the status of Moses is so deeply rooted in the faith of the people that it is becoming more difficult to refute him than the Exodus itself. It might be that the people could be formed without the event of Exodus. However, without the teaching of the man Moses they will lack the essence of their faith and the specific characteristics of their spirituality and morals as the nation of Israel.

Thus, it seems that in the discussion of Exodus and the creation of the Hebrew nation, there is a need to find a plausible explanation for the reality of Moses, with an effort to find support for his existence according to historical clues. It should be stated, however, in the beginning, that there is no intent to declare that this was the case in reality, but it is the author's judgement that there is stronger basis trying to support the existence of Moses than to abandon it, this is different from the case of Exodus itself.

Moses and the linkage to Egypt and Midian

The link between Moses, Midian, and Egypt is essential for understanding of his existence and actions. It may be said up front that the mythological story of the finding of Moses by the daughter of Pharaoh and its continuation is not plausible from its beginning. For the daughter of a pharaoh is by no means a graduate of the Hebrew Academy, able to invent an action-related name based on high knowledge of Hebrew: "And she called his name Moses, and said: 'Because I drew him out of the water'" [Mosheh for Meshitihu –וַתִּקְרָא שְׁמוֹ מֹשֶׁה כִּי מִן הַמַּיִם מְשִׁיתִהוּ] (Exod 2:10). In addition, it seems that regional traditions from the Near East have been adapted here, such as the legend of the survival of Sargon the elder, who established the dominant kingdom of Akkad (2400–2330 BCE), a story which is almost identical to that told of the newborn Moses: "And . . . she took for him an ark of bulrushes, and daubed it with slime and with pitch; and she put the child therein, and laid it in the flags by the river's brink" (Exod 2:3).

In relation to Exodus, the myth of the conflict between the Canaanites and the Egyptians may well be taken from the history of the Hyksos.[1] The central kingdom becomes weak in the "Second Intermediate period"—1640–1532 BCE. This state was exploited by people of mixed origins from the Near East, called Hyksos [Egyptian—"ruler(s) of the foreign countries"]. They settled in the eastern Nile Delta (Land of Goshen?), sometime before 1650 BCE, although immigration by Canaanite populations preceded the Hyksos, around 1800 BCE (Figure II.1).

---

1. Isserlin, *The Israelites*; Tiradritti, *Ancient Egypt*; Tubb, *Canaanites*.

Figure II.1: A tomb wall painting in Beni-Hasan, 1900 BCE showing a group of Canaanite shepherds in Egypt

They formed an independent state with its capital Avaris; its ruins are found today in Tel el-Dab'a. Eventually, Pharaoh Ahmose I waged war against the Hyksos and expelled them from Egypt circa 1550 BCE. The archeological findings showing architecture and paintings of the Minoan-Aegean culture similar to those found on Crete at the Palace of Knossos. Figure II.2, a wall painting from Avaris, the capitol of Hyksos in Egypt, sometimes mixed with Mediterranean, Syrian-Palestinian elements.

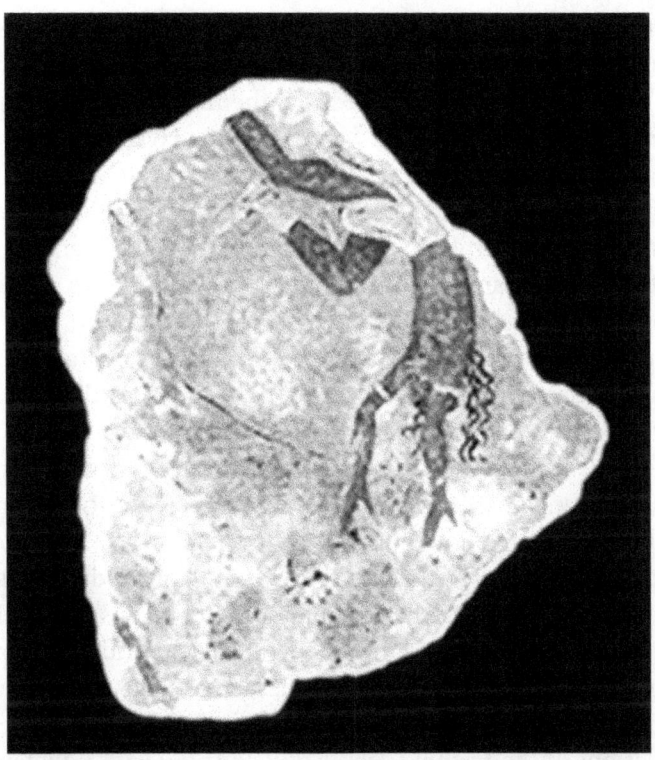

Figure II.2: Wall painting from Avaris, the capitol of Hyksos in Egypt, showing Minoan-Aegean culture

It is conceivable that the Hyksos were the Sea-people, like the Philistines, who together with groups of Canaanite origin arrived to Egypt and settled in the coastal area. Indeed, there is evidence of increased infiltration of Canaanites to the Nile Delta area even at the beginning of the second millennium BCE, the Middle Bronze Age. Of interest is the wall painting surviving from that time showing a group of Canaanite shepherds (Figure II.1). Maybe here can be found the significance of the Biblical sentence, as given by Joseph to his brethren "that ye shall say: Thy servants have been keepers of cattle from our youth even until now, both we, and our fathers; that ye may dwell in the land of Goshen; *for every shepherd is an abomination unto the Egyptians"* (Gen 46:34).

With the advent of the strengthening of Egyptian rule, Pharaoh Ahmose I waged war against the Hyksos and drove them from the Nile Delta region of Egypt, 1550–1525 BCE. The Egyptians drove them out and continued north (see map in Appendix), while conquering and destroying many cities in the Canaan area, circa 1550 BCE according to the archeological findings.[2] Gradually they took control of the land of Israel and eventually at about the fourteenth century BCE they annexed it as a colony, time that precedes that of the Judges (pre-monarchic era).[3]

It is conceivable that some of the escapees turned southeast of Canaan (Negev area of Israel) to the Transjordan area where they might join nomadic tribes such as the Midianites. These events may be the origin of the myth of Exodus including the struggle with the Egyptians.[4] A clue to this possibility may come from names in the Levi tribe (the tribe of Moses and Aaron), such as Hophni, Pinhas, and Merary, which first appeared as Egyptian names.[5] This may testify to the ancient relations of the Leviim (people of Levi tribe) with Egypt and of the Torah (teaching) of Moses with the Egyptian theology.

Another conceivable possibility is that some clergymen and their followers who had to flee Egypt because of the theological intolerance after the death of Pharaoh Amenhotep IV—Akhenaten (1355–1333 BCE), husband of the famous queen Nefertiti. This ruler tended to fanaticism for the monotheistic worship of the Sun god Aten. He transformed his name to Akhenaten (effective for Aten), giving the solar deity a status above mere gods and even built a new capital Akhetaten (now Amarna). After his death, his enterprise

2. Isserlin, *The Israelites*; Robins, *The Art of Ancient Egypt*; Tiradritti, *Ancient Egypt*; Tubb, *Canannites*.
3. Isserlin, *The Israelites*, 67; Tubb, *Canannites*.
4. Isserlin, *The Israelites*; Reade, *Mesopotamia*; Tubb, *Canaanites*,
5. Isserlin, *The Israelites*, 52.

collapsed, his monuments were dismantled and hidden, his statues were destroyed, and his name was not to be included in the kings list. It may well be that his followers, especially the theological ones, had to flee Egypt to other areas. It is of interest that chronologically this period could fit the appearance of Moses among the Israelite tribes, the beginning of the Judges era, considering the appearance of the kingdom circa the first millennium BCE.

Interestingly, this period of ruling the Land of Israel by Egypt is not mentioned at all in the books of the Torah, neither any event nor figure in the books of Torah is mentioned in Egyptian documents. This may testify that the mythos of Exodus, which is not mentioned by the Egyptians, evolved in a later time after Egypt left the land of Canaan.

It is of note that those communities such as Pithom and Ra'amses mentioned in the Hebrew Bible in relation to the Israelites' hard labor, did not exist at the time related to Exodus.[6] It is thus possible that the myth of the hard labor of the Hebrews in Egypt, like the myth of the newborn Moses' salvage, was based on general models, like the local one of the Kings David and Solomon in the building of the Temple, "And David commanded to gather together the strangers that were in the land of Israel; and he set masons to hew wrought stones to build the house of God" (1 Chr 1:22, 2). And later on:

> And Solomon numbered all the strangers that were in the land of Israel, after the numbering wherewith David his father had numbered them; and they were found a hundred and fifty thousand and three thousand and six hundred; And he set threescore and ten thousand of them to bear burdens, and fourscore thousand to be hewers in the mountains, and three thousand and six hundred overseers to set the people at work (2 Chr 2:16–17).

---

6. Reade, *Mesopotamia*, 52; Tubb, *Canaanites*.

"Overseers" here are parallel to the Egyptians taskmasters. "Therefore they did set over them taskmasters to afflict them with their burdens" mentioned in Exodus (Exod 1:11). It is possible that the writer had drawn a parallel between the realities in the land of Israel to that of the mythos of the hard labor of the Hebrews in Egypt, or perhaps this practice was common in the region as testified in some documents such as the stela of Mesha king of Moab (circa 840 BCE).

As will evolve later, the linkage with the ancient Egyptian theology is so essential that it is quite impossible to ignore. It is necessary to assume that this wide-range theology was known to the founder of the Hebrew faith, the man Moses and his followers, primarily the Levite clan. Theology that was implemented to the Hebrew tribes in the land of Canaan, who gradually evolved into a nation with its unique faith though worship and rituals, remained Canaanite by nature until the destruction of Jerusalem and the first temple (586 BCE). It is a basic point—as far as the historical knowledge and archeological facts enabling realization—that god YHWH—יְהוָה—was not known in the land of Canaan until the establishment of the Hebrew tribes on the Canaanite territories. This fits the detailed statement that He was not known to the forefathers, the Hebrew patriarchs, "and I appeared unto Abraham, unto Isaac, and unto Jacob, as God Almighty [El (god)—Shaday—אֵל שַׁדָּי], but by *My name YHWH I made Me not known to them*" (Exod 6:3). [In Hebrew language YHWH has no vowels and thus it is never pronounced, instead it is read as "Adonai"—i.e., Lord.]

Furthermore, unlike the gods of the Canaan region, Ba'al, Astrat-Ashtoret, Kemosh, Molekh, and others that were also worshiped by the Israelites, God YHWH—יְהוָה was not known or worshiped by any nation in the region. It could be inferred, therefore, that the origin of God YHWH—יְהוָה was not Canaanite or of northern nations, Aram, Tyre [צוּר], or Sidon for example, but from other areas (see below). Another supportive evidence is that it is not found in the names from that time is the suffix at the end of names "YAH—"יה, part of the God name יְהֹוָה, which was highly prevalent at later time in the names of kings or prophets, Uriah, Yoshyah—Josiah, Tsidkiah—Zedekiah, Yeshayah—Isaiah, Yermiyah—Jeremiah, and more.

From all the given clues, it may be conceivable to assume that Moses himself is of Semitic origin or even a Hebrew, although when presenting the god who sent him to the people of Israel he is saying "The LORD, the God of your fathers, the God of Abraham, of Isaac, and of Jacob, hath appeared unto me" (Exod 3:16), rather than—The God of *our* fathers, as should be appropriate. This relation of God seems to come to Moses after the definitive character of God, the Divine name YHWH—יְהֹוָה, was revealed to him—in the burning bush. Only in addressing the people of Israel is he attributing the god who had imposed on him the mission, to the ancient God of their forefathers, Shaday—שַׁדַּי. Again, it is conceivable that Moses himself was of Semitic or Hebrew origin; otherwise, it would be difficult to assume that his spiritual mission and leadership would be accepted by the Israelites.

The sojourn of Moses in Egypt is also a difficult matter for the lack of support or a historical clue, except for the surprising similarity between the new faith offered by him to that of ancient Egypt (see chapter IV). This parallelism is so profound, showing a wide knowledge and mastering that would come only after long interaction. Such an influence might be related to the long stay of the Hyksos in Egypt, who were expelled back to the land of Canaan as discussed above.

As for the spiritual relations, the script itself is indicating the long stay of Moses in Midian, a desert area close to Egypt. It is of note that he dwelt with the chief priest of Midian, Jethro—יִתְרוֹ, whose daughter he married, "And Moses was content to dwell with the man; and he (the priest of Midian) gave Moses Zipporah his daughter" (Exod 2:21). It is of special significance that both the theological recognition of the new Divine entity YHWH—יְהֹוָה and his mission came to Moses during his stay in Midian. There, in his long journeys in the desert as a shepherd, the recognition of God and the plan of his mission came to him—as described in the revelation of God in the burning bush,

> *And the angel of the LORD appeared unto him in a flame of fire out of the midst of a bush; and he looked, and, behold, the bush burned with fire, and the bush was not consumed ... And the LORD said ... 'Come now therefore, and I will send thee unto Pharaoh, that thou mayest bring forth My people the children of Israel out of Egypt' (Exod 2-10).*

It is also clear that the plan of Exodus had already matured in his vision at that time. Moses knew where the revelation of God to the people is going to be, "when thou hast brought forth the people out of Egypt, ye shall serve God upon this mountain" (Exod 3:12). A mountain that he arrived at during his wandering in the desert, a mountain where he will provide the people with the Ten Commandments. It seems that even the geographic destination was also chosen at that time "... and to bring them up out of that land (Egypt) ... unto the place of the Canaanite ..." (Exod 3:8).

Historical evidence is supported by findings that the Midianite were a nomadic tribe in the south-east of the Land of Israel, in areas that are bordered with Egypt, which controlled the south and even the northern areas of the land for a long time. Further:

1. The most startling fact is that while the absolute lack of YHWH -יְהֹוָה worship in the area of Canaan prior to the establishment of the Hebrew tribes (fourteenth-thirteenth century BCE), the name YHWH—יְהֹוָה was already found in Midian. It seems therefore that it was exported from there to the north to the Hebrew tribes in the land of Canaan.[7] Indeed, in two Egyptian texts

---

7. Isserlin, *The Israelites*, 53.

from the fourteenth-thirteenth centuries BCE (prior to the Judges era), the name יְהוָֹה appears in relation to the south Transjordan area where the Midianites dwelled. In another document, the name YHWH—יְהוָֹה of Teiman (Edom—south Transjordan) is mentioned. Another testimony could be found in the ancient "Song of Deborah", which is related to the thirteenth-twelfth century BCE prior to the kingdom in the tenth century BCE, "LORD, when Thou didst go forth out of Seir, when Thou didst march out of the field of Edom" (Judg 5:4), and the old "Ha'azinu" (hearken) poem, called "Moses Song", "The LORD came from Sinai, and rose from Seir unto them" (Deut 33:2). Edom and Seir are related to the south Transjordan area, where the Midianite used to live. It seems therefore that the origin of the faith in YHWH came from south-east to the Land of Israel. This is in contrast to all the divine entities worshiped by the Hebrews, which originated in the north, the land of Canaan, Syrian-Aramaic, or Phoenician as mentioned. It may be worth noting here that Mount Sinai, the mount of God revelation, should be in that area of Transjordan as the ancient scripts indicate, rather than in the Sinai Peninsula as many believe; for example, Saint Catherine's Monastery, the "Sacred Monastery of the God-Trodden Mount Sinai" administered by the Eastern Orthodox Church.

2. Another surprising finding is that the Midianites used a portable shrine covered by a tent, as shown by archeological findings in Timna, in the south of Israel, similar in structure to the Tabernacle described in the book of Exodus,

> *According to all that I show thee, the pattern of the tabernacle, and the pattern of all the furniture thereof, even so shall ye make it; And every wise-hearted man ... made the tabernacle with ten curtains: of fine twined linen, and blue, and purple, and scarlet;*

> *And he made curtains of goats' hair for a tent over the tabernacle; eleven curtains he made them; And he made a covering for the tent of rams' skins dyed red, and a covering of sealskins above (Exod 36:14-19).*

This is around 1,200BCE, about the time the Hebrew tribes organized into a political entity, around the late bronze age.[8]

3. An amazing finding is the relic of the brass serpent in the Midianite portable shrine, similar to which Moses made and erected in the Tabernacle: "And Moses made a serpent of brass, and set it upon the pole" (Num 21:9). An artifact that continues to exist in the Tabernacle in Shilo, the old worship site in the Land of Israel. It is of great interest that this object, which represents a secondary god named Nehushta—נְחֻשְׁתָּן [Serpent in Hebrew is Nahash—נָחָשׁ] survived to the late era of King Hezekiah of Judah (circa eighth-seventh centuries BCE), who made wide religious reform for restoring the worship of YHWH—יְהוָה. During that reform he broke the brass serpent that was an object of worship among people, "... and he broke in pieces the brazen serpent that Moses had made; for unto those days the children of Israel did offer to it; and it was called Nehushtan" [serpent in Hebrew Nahash—נָחָשׁ], (2 Kgs 18:4). (Figure II.3).

---

8. Isserlin, *The Israelites*; Reade, *Mesopotamia*; Tubb, *Canaanites*.

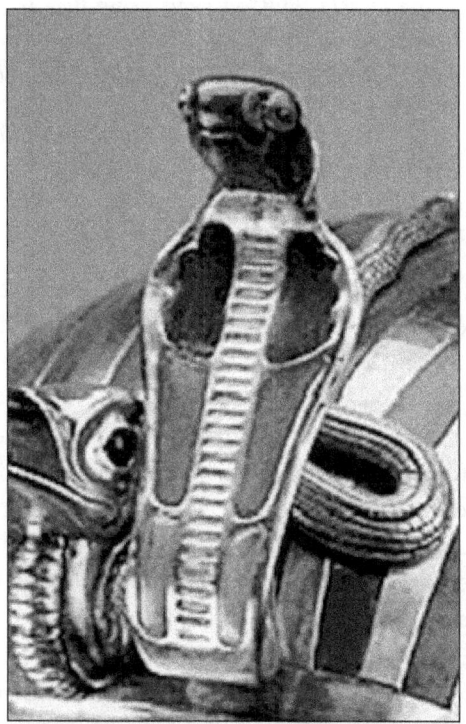

Figure II.3 Mask of Tutankhamun featuring a Uraeus, symbol for protection

In summary, it appears that the faith in YHWH—יְהֹוָה was imported from the south-east by a man who knew it profoundly and introduced it systematically, with the help of the Levite clan and the priest's organization, his tribe, and family. Although this is an evolutionary process as history shows, it became the exclusive faith of the social-political entity as it gradually crystalized in the land of Canaan. An entity in formation that was seeking exclusive characteristics for self-identification. Indeed, between the Hebrew tribes and God YHWH –יְהֹוָה a mutual covenant was formed, He chose His people, and they chose Him as their unique God. Following the categorical ordinance "Thou shalt have no other gods before Me" (Exod 20:2), God is further ordering that

The Origin of the Hebrews and Their Faith

> *When the LORD thy God shall bring thee into the land whither thou goest to possess it . . . ye shall break down their altars, and dash in pieces their pillars, and hew down their Asherim, and burn their graven images with fire, For thou art a holy people unto the LORD thy God: the LORD thy God hath chosen thee to be His own treasure, out of all peoples that are upon the face of the earth (Deut 7:1–6).*

And God, as mentioned, contracts an alliance with the chosen people "And I will . . . be your God, and ye shall be My people" (Lev 26:12).

Back to the remarkable man Moses. His relations with the Midianites is long-lasting and significant. "And afterward the people . . . pitched in the wilderness of Paran" (Num 12:16), their wandering did occur in the area of these people and where the remnants of the portable shrine, the "Tabernacle", were found, Paran desert. Jethro, the Mianite chief priest and the father-in-law of Moses, is in close contact, according to the script, "Now Jethro, the priest of Midian, Moses' father-in-law, heard of all that God had done for Moses, . . . And Jethro . . . came with his sons and his wife (of Moses) unto Moses into the wilderness where he was encamped, *at the mount of God*" (Exod 18:1–5). And he is advising Moses how to mediate between the People and their God, as the tradition of the clergymen in all civilizations along history, "Hearken now unto my voice, I will give thee counsel, and God be with thee: be thou for the people before God, and bring thou the causes unto God", "So Moses hearkened to the voice of his father-in-law, and did all that he had said" (Exod 18:19–24).

And the mediation task was highly successful, "And they said unto Moses: 'Speak thou with us, and we will hear; but let not God speak with us, lest we die . . . And the people stood afar off; but Moses drew near unto the thick darkness where God was" (Exod 20:16-18), and again "and Moses alone shall come near unto the LORD; but they shall not come near; neither shall the people go up with him".

And following that mission, "And Moses came and told the people all the words of the LORD, and all the ordinances; and all the people answered with one voice, and said: 'All the words which the LORD hath spoken (from the mouth of Moses) will we do'" (Exod 24:2-3).

There are two remarkable events in that meeting that require comments. First, "And Jethro, Moses' father-in-law, took a burnt-offering and sacrifices for God ..." (Exod 18:12). This event implies that Jethro the Midianite Chief Priest recognized that God as a legitimate deity for worship, and maybe it was he who passed that recognition to Moses himself.

Second, Jethro the Chief Priest of Midian is meeting with Moses at the Mountain of God; a meeting that is immediately followed by the revelation of God to the people of Israel and the delivery to them of the Ten Commandments by Moses. The revelation of God in the Paran wilderness and the relation to Midian is echoed many years later, "God cometh from Teman (south), and the Holy One from mount Paran ... and there is the hiding of His power" (Hab 3:3-4), and "the curtains of the land of Midian do tremble (from the appearance of God)" (Hab 3:7).

And even after the remarkable theological event of God's revelation the ties with the Midianites continued, "And Moses said unto Hobab, the son of Reuel the Midianite ... : 'We are journeying unto the place of which the LORD said: I will give it you; come thou with us, and we will do thee good; for the LORD hath spoken good concerning Israel", and "... And he (Moses) said: 'Leave us not, I pray thee; forasmuch as thou knowest how we are to encamp in the wilderness, and thou shalt be to us instead of eyes'", "And they set forward from the mount of the LORD ... and the ark of the covenant of the LORD went before them (Num 10:29-33). Again here the relations with the Midianites are emphasized, the people who led Moses and his group into their final destination.

A quite surprising testimony for the linkage between the Midianites and the people of Israel is found later in the Book of Judges, at the time the people were settling in the land of Canaan, "And the children of ... Moses' father-in-law, went up out of the city of palm-trees (Jericho) with the children of Judah into the wilderness of Judah, which is in the south of Arad; and they went and dwelt with the people" (Judg 1:16). It seems that the Midianites, the relatives of Moses, were finally incorporated into the people of Israel, a testimony that strengthens the idea regarding the origin of Moses and his theology.

Highly convincing evidence for the association of Moses and his group who came out of the country to the people living in Canaan ("Israeli tribes") is the fact that of all the tribes, only the tribe of the Levites, the family of Moses himself, doesn't have land for settlement in the land of Canaan. This fact strongly indicates that this group immigrated to a land that had been already occupied by other people, the "tribes of Israel". Thus, there were given cities and lands for inhabitation in the heritage of the other tribes, "and they gave no portion unto the Levites in the land, save cities to dwell in, with the open land about them for their cattle and for their substance. As the LORD commanded Moses, so the children of Israel did" (Josh 14:4–5). It is undoubtedly remarkable that the Levites, the immediate tribe of Moses himself, the almighty leader by his order, as the script indicates, the settlements were given to the various tribes, lacks a land for itself. It seems clear then that this group did not possess any settlement in the Land of Canaan, and thus could not claim a land as the other tribes did. Had the Levites had land it would be highly improbable to deprive them of it, especially at the time of the tribal settlement.

Here maybe finally it is possible to find the basis for understanding of the relations between Moses, Exodus, and the Hebrew tribes. As mentioned, the origin of the faith in God YHWH—יְהוָה and the portable shrine, the Tabernacle [Hebrew: Mishkan מִשְׁכָּן, a place for dwelling], is in the south-east desert, the land of nomad tribes as the Midianites were. It seems from the circumstances described in the scripture that Moses was a leader of a group, possibly of Hebrew or other Semitic origin, that was wandering in the desert, joined the Midianites and adopted from them the new theology, especially since Moses himself dwelled with the Midianites' chief priest and became his son-in-law. Later on, they wandered to the fertile land of Canaan and integrated with the Hebrew population who were there, providing theological and teaching service, as the scripture indicates. This scenario can also explain why this group had so much difficulty struggling with other ethnic groups in their way north, such as the Amalekite, people of Arad, Edom, Moab, and Amon, and thus, had, as the script testifies, to surround the land and to come from East. This group had grown over time, and only when they later joined the "Hebrew" tribes could they integrate with them as spiritual-social leaders in the settlement process as described in Scripture,

> Now the children of Reuben and the children of Gad had a very great multitude of cattle; and when they saw the land of Jazer, and the land of Gilead, that, behold, the place was a place for cattle, the children of Gad and the children of Reuben came and spoke unto Moses, and to Eleazar the priest, and unto the princes of the congregation, saying: 'Ataroth, and Dibon, and Jazer, and Nimrah, and Heshbon, and Elealeh, and Sebam, and Nebo, and Beon, the land which the LORD smote before the congregation of Israel, is a land for cattle, and thy servants have cattle' (Num 32:1–5).

The offer of spiritual-religious leadership was essential to this group of tribal families who were in a process of social organizational and political convergence while taking over Canaanite territories. A group that was in the process of needing strong spiritual support, a God of its own with unique spiritual characteristics to help crystallize the emerging society. This possibility may explain both the wandering in the desert of the group of people under the leadership of Moses and the possible confrontation with the Egyptians who ruled for a long time in the south of Canaan (see the remains of an Egyptian temple in the Timna area in the south of Israel). It is also possible that the stories of the Hyksos, of Canaanite people who were expelled from the land of Egypt and who found temporary refuge with the Midianites in the desert, created the myth of the exodus from Egypt. A myth that was delivered and later written down by the same priests—Levites—who imported it into the land of Canaan.

The possibility that Moses himself was an Egyptian man who wandered into the Midianite tribes' region is less likely. The idolatry of Egypt was well-known and well-documented, and it is therefore very surprising that the new worship of God YHWH—יְהֹוָה proposed by Moses and the Levites to the tribes in Canaan does not have any Egyptian ceremonial component. On the contrary, all the worship of God is essentially similar to that in the region of Canaan and the north, with its variety of regional gods that were also worshiped by the Israelites during the First Temple period (ninth to sixth centuries BCE), as the scripture testifies. In addition, it is hard to conceive the acceptance of a man of Ham descent as a spiritual leader to the Semitic tribes.

The question of the strong similarity between ancient Egyptian theology and that of Moses' monotheism can also be explained (see chapter IV). The Midianite tribes in the south were undoubtedly in constant contact with the Egyptians whose temple remains were found not only in the Timna Valley in the Arava (south of Israel), but even in northern areas, according to the archaeological findings. A monotheistic spiritual theology, purer than the idolatry practiced in the rich temples of Egypt, was more suited to a wandering desert people with very limited means.

Here in the wilderness, in contrast to the rich fertile land of Egypt, a simple religion could emerge, satisfied with a single major god who also has no image, which alleviates the need to prepare visual figures that require the construction of statues, temples, and sacrifices.

It may well be that from here came the abstraction of God as manifested in the Ten Commandments: "Thou shalt not make unto thee a graven image, nor any manner of likeness, of anything that is in heaven above, or that is in the earth beneath, or that is in the water under the earth; thou shalt not bow down unto them, nor serve them" (Exod 20:3–4).

Chapter III

The Settlement in the Land of Canaan

The New God

THE PROCESS OF INTEGRATION of the tribes and their settlement in the land of Canaan was accompanied by the adoption of an exclusive supreme power that would follow and support the chosen group in their long, difficult, and challenging task.

Evidence of the adoption of the new God in the early period in which the tribal coalition began to crystallize, is found in the ancient text of the "Song of Deborah" (attributed to the thirteenth to twelfth century BCE). There, the people's satisfaction with the chosen God's work in overcoming a powerful enemy, such as Yabin the Canaanite king of Hazor and the captain of his army Sisera, is expressed,

> LORD, when Thou didst go forth out of Seir, when Thou didst march out of the field of Edom, the earth trembled, the heavens also dropped, yea, the clouds dropped water. The mountains quaked at the presence of the LORD, even Sinai at the presence of the LORD, the God of Israel. (Judg 5, 4-5). The rulers

ceased in Israel, they ceased, until that thou didst arise, Deborah, that thou didst arise a mother in Israel. They (Israel) chose new god . . . Bless ye the LORD (Judg 5, 7-9).

The choice of God by the people is also emphasized in the Book of Joshua, after the initial settlement, "And Joshua said unto the people: 'Ye are witnesses against yourselves that *ye have chosen you the LORD*, to serve Him . . . And they said: 'We are witnesses'" (Josh 24, 22).

Interestingly, here is the obvious hint that the chosen God indeed came from the south—the mountain of Seir in the land of Edom. Further, Mount Sinai, the place of God revelation and the delivery of his commandments and statute [Hebrew "Matan—Torah", giving of Law] is also located there. The location is emphasized again in the ancient "Song of Moses" [Hebrew—Song of Ha'azinu, hearken], "And he said: The LORD came from Sinai, and rose from Seir unto them" (Deut 33, 2).

This is in accordance with mentioning the name YHWH in ancient Egyptian documents from the fourteenth and thirteenth centuries BCE (before or at the beginning of the Judges period) to the region of Transjordan to the south, where the Midianites lived.[1] It is significant that the first contact of the wandering group of Moses in the desert is with the inhabitants of the south, Edom and Arad in the Negev (Num 21: 1). It is also interesting that the ritual object, the brass serpent found in the Midianite tabernacle, was also made by Moses in the south on the border of Edom, "And they journeyed . . . to compass the land of Edom; And Moses made a serpent of brass, and set it upon the pole" (Num 21: 4, 9).

Note: In Egyptian documents, the name of the place Y-H-W is mentioned in the south-east Transjordan area;[2] thus, it is possible that some of the people who were later identified with the Israelites or the Levites, the tribe of Moses, came

1. Isserlin, *The Israelites*.
2. *Ibid.*

from there. It should be noted that even the text itself indicates that the wanderers were a heterogeneous group: "And a mixed multitude went up also with them" (Exod 12:38).

In the context of the consolidation of the tribes, it is worth noting that in the "Song of Deborah", the name of the mighty tribe of Judah is absent from the list of fighting tribes mentioned there, probably as evidence that the southern tribe Judah, associated with the Moabites, was not yet integrated into the evolving Israeli coalition, which was completed only under the severe pressure of the Philistines.

The chosen God who is now needed for the emerging society is a warrior god who will assist his people in their long and difficult mission of conquering the land of Canaan,

> *Then sang Moses and the children of Israel this song unto the LORD, and spoke, saying: . . . The LORD is my strength . . . and He is become my salvation . . . The LORD is a man of war, YHWH is His name . . . Thy right hand, O LORD, glorious in power, Thy right hand, O LORD, dasheth in pieces the enemy. And in the greatness of Thine excellency Thou overthrowest them that rise up against Thee; Thou sendest forth Thy wrath, it consumeth them as stubble (Exod 15, 1-7).*

For comparison, note the Ugarit text "Here are your enemies, Baal, your enemies you will crush".[3]

The features of the chosen God as a powerful warrior who is able to help his people succeed even against overwhelming forces is further highlighted in the last book of the Torah, "*I will make Mine arrows drunk with blood, and My sword shall devour flesh*" (Deut 32, 42). The status of God as a super-warrior of the people is emphasized many times in the context of the conquest of the land and the tribal expansion: "And Moses went and spoke these words unto all Israel. The LORD thy God, He will go over before thee; He will destroy these nations from before thee, and thou shalt dispossess

---

3. Darshan and Darshan, *Canaanite Mythology*.

them" (Deut 31, 1-3). And following the success: "Happy art thou, O Israel, who is like unto thee? a people saved by *the LORD*, the shield of thy help, and that *is the sword* of thy excellency!" (Deut 33, 29).

The practical use of God in fighting the enemy is well-described in three events in which God is presented through the Ark of Covenant, which holds the "Tablets of Commandment" לֻחֹת הַבְּרִית,—meaning the tablets of the covenant. One is the miraculous passage of the overflowing Jordan River by Joshua and the people, "And it shall come to pass, when the soles of the feet of the priests that bear the ark of the LORD, the Lord of all the earth, shall rest in the waters of the Jordan, that the waters of the Jordan shall be cut off, even the waters that come down from above; and they shall stand in one heap" (Josh 3, 13). This miracle allowed the people crossing the Jordan on their way to inherit the land.

The second event is the conquest of Jericho. "And Joshua rose early in the morning, and the priests took up the ark of the LORD. And the seven priests bearing the seven rams' horns before the ark of the LORD ... And ... they compassed the city" (Josh 6,12-14). Then came the success, "And ... when the people heard the sound of the horn, that the people shouted with a great shout, and the wall (of Jericho) fell down flat, so that the people went up ... and they took the city" (Josh 6, 20).

While these two events were quite successful, the third attempt, using the Ark of Covenant for the war against the Philistines, ended in unfavorable results and with great embarrassment: "And the man said unto Eli (the Chief Priest): ' ... I fled to-day out of the army ... 'Israel is fled before the Philistines, and there hath been also a great slaughter among the people ... *and the ark of God is taken*" (Samuel I 4, 16-17).

Back to the settlement era—it seems that the gradual takeover of the Canaanite land while eliminating its residents required strong authority with ideological and theological support. It is no coincidence that the right to inherit the land is vested by the same divine entity that was established for the occupying people—the Lord YHWH—יְהוָֹה. It probably wouldn't be possible to use the gods of the surrounding regions that had been already adopted by the other nations. For example, the adoption of the warrior god Ba'al by the peoples of the North: "Behold, your enemies Ba'al, your enemies you will crush". Here, very instructive for the role of God to endow a living space for his people, are the words of the Judge Jephthah יִפְתָּח—Yiftah of the Gilead to the King of Ammon: "So now the LORD, the God of Israel, hath dispossessed the Amorites from before His people Israel. Wilt not thou possess that which Chemosh thy god giveth thee to possess? So whomsoever the LORD our God hath dispossessed from before us, them will we possess" (Judg 11, 23-24).

This claim is an echo of the promised divine grant already mentioned in the Book of Joshua, "[and] the LORD spoke unto Joshua the son of Nun ... go over this Jordan, thou, and all this people, unto the land which I do give to them, even to the children of Israel. Every place that the sole of your foot shall tread upon, to you have I given it" (Josh 1, 1-3)

YHWH—יְהוָֹה is the exclusive God who rose to the evolving group of people and provided the legitimacy of conquering the land from all its inhabitants. This is mentioned even, as the scripture tells, in the period of Moses, the man of God,

> and Og the king of Bashan went out against them, he and all his people, to battle at Edrei. And the LORD said unto Moses: 'Fear him not; for I have delivered him into thy hand, and all his people, and his land; and thou shalt do to him as thou didst unto Sihon king of the Amorites, who dwelt at Heshbon.' So they smote him, and his sons, and all his people, until there was none left him remaining; and they possessed his land (Num 21, 33-34).

The Settlement in the Land of Canaan

And Joshua is following the Divine order, "So the people shouted, and [the priests] blew with the horns . . . and they took the city [Jericho]. And they utterly destroyed all that was in the city, both man and woman, both young and old, and ox, and sheep, and ass, with the edge of the sword" (Josh 6, 20-21).

And God, the Lord of war, continues His command: "And the LORD said unto Joshua: . . . see, I have given into thy hand the king of Ai, and his people, and his city, and his land. And thou shalt do to Ai and her king as thou didst unto Jericho and her king" (Josh 8, 1-2). And Joshua kept following the order for the entire land, and at the end of the war, "So Joshua smote all the land, the hill-country, and the South, and the Lowland, and the slopes, and all their kings; he left none remaining; but he utterly destroyed all that breathed, as the LORD, the God of Israel, commanded" (Josh 10,40). And finally, "So Joshua took the whole land, according to all that the LORD spoke unto Moses; and Joshua gave it for an inheritance unto Israel according to their divisions by their tribes. And the land had rest from war" (Josh 11, 23).

It is no coincidence that the most active leader in occupying the land as is told, repeatedly emphasizes the coalition with YHWH—יְהוָה to grant full legitimacy to the conquest of the land. Finally, he gathered all the people to make a covenant with YHWH—יְהוָה, to worship him and to obey all his commands,

> And Joshua gathered all the tribes of Israel to Shechem, and called for the elders of Israel, and for their heads, and for their judges, and for their officers; and they presented themselves before God . . . saying 'and now therefore fear the LORD, and serve Him' . . . And the people answered and said: 'Far be it from us that we should forsake the LORD, to serve other gods;
> And Joshua said unto the people:
> Ye are witnesses against yourselves that ye have chosen you the LORD, to serve Him.—And they said:

> 'We are witnesses.'—*And the people said unto Joshua: 'The LORD our God will we serve, and unto His voice will we hearken.' So Joshua made a covenant with the people that day, and set them a statute and an ordinance in Shechem. And Joshua wrote these words in the book of the law of God* (Josh 24, 1, 14, 16, 22, 24-26).

Indeed, the combination of spiritual-theological backing with the act of the conquest itself has finally created the social-political entity that was hoped for by Moshe, the Master of the Prophets, who even foresaw that "When thou art come unto the land which the LORD thy God giveth thee, and shalt possess it, and shalt dwell therein ... thou shalt set a king over thee, whom the LORD thy God shall choose" (Deut 17, 14-15).

Hence the religious legitimization of the chosen king by the Man of God. This is performed by the ceremonial action of the anointment by the priest [Cohen—כֹּהֵן] of YHWH—יְהֹוָה. From here came the term "Anointed of God"—Meshiach Adonai –מְשִׁיחַ יְהוָה [to anoint in Hebrew—Limshoach—למשוח], and the title "מָשִׁיחַ"—Mashiach, or "Messiah" in the Greek translation, which later became rooted in the Western tradition.

It is of prime importance to note that now when resting from war, the attributes of God are transformed into those that the people needed for the foundation of a just and compassionate social order: "And the LORD passed by before him (Moses), and proclaimed: 'The LORD, the LORD, God, *merciful* and *gracious, long-suffering,* and *abundant in goodness and truth*'" (Exod 34, 6).

The God revealed here is a God with highly developed moral-social messages that are summed up in his commandments: "*Thou shalt love thy neighbour as thyself:* I am the LORD" (Lev 19, 18); and, "*Justice, justice shalt thou pursue*" (Deut 16, 20). Commands and statutes that became the

THE SETTLEMENT IN THE LAND OF CANAAN

pillars of the ethical orientation and the social order inherited by the entire Western civilization.

The integration of the tribes and the conquest of the land—The books of Joshua and Judges

Another issue that is rather crucial in discussing the Exodus from Egypt and the consolidation of the Hebrew people is the story of the conquest of the land of Canaan. It should be stated immediately at the beginning, that not only the historical and archaeological evidence, such as the fact that Jericho was destroyed hundreds of years before the proposed event of its capture by the Israelites (see below), but also the organization of the tribes in the desert, as described, and the subsequent events do not support the story of organized occupation.

The organization of wandering tribes in the desert is described as an impressive military array. Each tribe is a tight unit, carries their flag or standard, and camps in a defined oriented location. In order to have a direct impression on the organization, here is the entire passage from Numbers chapter 2, which describes the military array, camping orientation, name of the commander and the number of his armed soldiers.

> *The children of Israel shall pitch by their fathers' houses; every man with his own standard, according to the ensigns; a good way off shall they pitch round about the tent of meeting [the Tabernacle, Mishkan, a portable shrine] (Num 2, 2)."*

"Now those that pitch on the east side toward the sunrising shall be they of the standard of the camp of *Judah*, according to their hosts; the prince of the children of Judah being Nahshon the son of Amminadab,[4] and his host . . . threescore and

---

4. Some of the names of the chiefs of the tribes contain the theophoric prefix El (God, the ancient god in the land of Canaan, Eliab, Elishamah) or

fourteen thousand and six hundred. The tribe of *Issachar* fifty and four thousand and four hundred, the tribe of *Zebulun* fifty and seven thousand and four hundred, the tribe of *Reuben* hundred thousand and fifty and one thousand and four hundred and fifty, according to their hosts; and they shall set forth second; the tribe of *Simeon* fifty and nine thousand and three hundred; and the tribe of *Gad* forty and five thousand and six hundred and fifty; the camp of *Ephraim*, forty thousand and five hundred; the tribe of *Manasseh* thirty and two thousand and two hundred; the tribe of *Benjamin* thirty and five thousand and four hundred; and in summary: These are they that were numbered of the children of Israel by their fathers' houses; *all that were numbered of the camps* according to their hosts were *six hundred thousand and three thousand and five hundred and fifty*".

This is undoubtedly a mighty army, especially in those days (thirteenth-twelfth century BCE). But what happens next? This vast array is attacked by a nomadic tribe (the Amalekites) and cannot manage. The problem is so grave that a special commandment is given from God to announce and even put in writing that the memory of Amalek must be erased from under heaven, "And the LORD said unto Moses: 'Write this for a memorial in the book, and rehearse it in the ears of Joshua: for I will utterly blot out the remembrance of Amalek from under heaven'" (Exod 17, 14); and at the end of the Torah a reminder from God, "Remember what Amalek did unto thee by the way as ye came forth out of Egypt; ... Therefore it shall be, when the LORD thy God hath given thee rest from all thine enemies round about, ... that thou shalt blot out the remembrance of Amalek from under heaven; thou shalt not forget" (Deut 25, 17-19).

---

suffix of Shadai, Tsur-Shadai, Shdeur, the name of the ancient god who was revealed to the forefathers Abraham, Isaac, and Jacob, but not the prefix Yah or Yeho related to YHWH the god who was revealed to Moses, which testifies for its old origin. See below on Exodus and Moses.

The Settlement in the Land of Canaan

A second event from the period of wandering in the desert is the war with the Moabites, which is also not indicative of great strength. Therefore, this detailed chapter of the Israeli military assembly is undoubtedly derived from a later period, the time of the monarchy, in which all the tribes joined together to fight a common enemy, most probably the Philistines. This chapter seems therefore unintentionally extended to the story of wandering in the desert by the editor who operated at later time, as mentioned.

The critical reader should note that such errors of anachronism and misplacement are not rare, and that they may be found elsewhere in the text, for example, in the thanksgiving prayer of Hannah, which is nothing more than a song of thanks for the king's victory over his enemies: "And Hannah prayed, and said: my heart exulteth in the LORD, my horn (strength) is exalted in the LORD; my mouth is enlarged over mine enemies; because I rejoice in Thy salvation . . . and He will give strength unto His king, and exalt the horn of His anointed (1 Sam 2, 1-10).

Another famous example is the "Song of the Sea", which is supposed to take place immediately after the passage of the Red Sea as stated, "Then sang Moses and the children of Israel this song unto the LORD, and spoke, saying: 'I will sing unto the LORD, for He is highly exalted; the horse and his rider hath He thrown into the sea'"(Exod 15, 1). However, later on comes the story of the arrival to the promised land and the establishment of the Temple, "Thou bringest them in, and plantest them in the mountain of Thine inheritance, the place, O LORD, which Thou hast made for Thee to dwell in, the sanctuary [Temple], O Lord, which Thy hands have established" (Exod 15, 17).

And back to the chapter of the military arrangement, "shall they pitch round about the tent of meeting [Ohel Mo'ed, Tabernacle, Mishkan, a portable shrine]" (Num 2, 2). If the critical reader would continue asking what is the matter of the Ohel Mo'ed in a war, it should be noted that in ancient times God's primary role was to protect the city or state that adopted him, a tradition that lasted until the modern era in Western culture, where every city has a patron, a Christian saint; many of the cities are still named after him. The God of Israel at that time "The LORD is a man of war, YHWH is his name" (Exod 15, 3). Thus, it was customary to have the divine power participating in wars, as in the description of the conquest of Jericho, where the priests with the Holy Ark are leading, a story which resulted in success. Then, the shameful story of the Holy Ark being taken by the Philistines on the battlefield:

> *And there ran a man of Benjamin out of the army, and came to Shiloh [where the Mishkan, the temporary temple used to be] with his clothes rent, and with earth upon his head . . . and the man said unto Eli [the Chief Priest] . . . I fled to-day out of the army, Israel is fled before the Philistines, and there hath been also a great slaughter among the people, and thy two sons [Priests] also, Hophni and Phinehas, are dead, and the ark of God is taken (1 Sam 4, 12-17).*

However, the main questions of conquest appear within the country. The events here are not as expected from a massive and orderly military array as described earlier. Immediately after the description of an organized and successful war against the various 31 kings (rulers of cities/states), suddenly appears a completely different historical description. The same military organization disappeared and is replaced by individual tribes separately fighting the inhabitants of the land. The individual tribes sometimes form a narrow *ad hoc* coalition to fight a common enemy, or in return for aid to the joining tribe. This realistic description is found in the Book of Judges, and there is almost no possibility but to present only a few examples: "And Judah said unto Simeon his brother: 'Come up with me into my lot, that we may fight against the Canaanites; and I likewise will go with thee into

The Settlement in the Land of Canaan

thy lot.' So Simeon went with him" (Judg 1, 3). And then the conquest of Safed: "And Judah went with Simeon his brother, and they smote the Canaanites that inhabited Zephath". A very impressive socio-cultural aspect is the story of the conquest of Kiryat Sefer, where the promised reward for the hero who conquers the city is the daughter of the Chief of the tribe: "And Caleb [the Chief of the mighty tribe Judah—Yehudah] said: 'He that smiteth Kiriath-sepher, and taketh it, to him will I give Achsah my daughter to wife.'" And Judah is doing well even on his own in the southern region, and no wonder the continuation of the monarchy was attributed to him [King David's dynasty]:

> *And afterward the children of Judah went down to fight against the Canaanites that dwelt in the hill-country, and in the South, and in the Lowland. Also, Judah took Gaza with the border thereof, and Ashkelon with the border thereof, and Ekron with the border thereof. And the LORD was with Judah; and he drove out the inhabitants of the hill-country.*

And the other tribes as well. "And the house of Joseph, they also went up against Beth-el; and the LORD was with them, and they smote the city with the edge of the sword."

But there are also failures, especially without assistance: "And the children of Benjamin did not drive out the Jebusites that inhabited Jerusalem; but the Jebusites dwelt with the children of Benjamin in Jerusalem, unto this day" (Josh 2, 63).

And thereafter is presented a very long list of failures, with the conclusion of that period: "And it came to pass, when Israel was waxen strong, that they put the Canaanites to task-work, but did in no wise drive them out" (Judg I, 28).

In conclusion, this description of tribes acting alone and creating limited coalitions when needed, *ad hoc* coalitions, undoubtedly reflects more faithfully the gradual takeover of the Canaanite people by the Hebrew tribes than the mythical-heroic story of exodus from Egypt and the organized one-time conquest of the land.

In further reading, the text is leaving no doubt that such wars also occurred between the Hebrew tribes themselves. For the reader's convenience, here are only two examples.

Ephraim, the dominant tribe, also seeks their share in the achievements: "And the men of Ephraim were gathered together, and passed to Zaphon; and they said unto Jephthah (Yiftach): 'Wherefore didst thou pass over to fight against the children of Ammon, and didst not call us to go with thee? we will burn thy house upon thee with fire'" (Judg 12, 1). But here the strong tribe did not correctly assess the strength of the victorious Yiftach who was called to save the inhabitants of Gilad from the Ammonites: "Then Jephthah gathered together all the men of Gilead, and fought with Ephraim; and the men of Gilead smote Ephraim, ... and there fell at that time of Ephraim forty and two thousand" (Judg 12, 4-6).

The second prominent episode is the war against the Benjaminites, which almost destroyed the tribe of Benjamin and later an extraordinary and highly imaginative means needed to rehabilitate it. As described in the Book of Judges chapter 20, a heavy and professional corps of sword and stone fighters:

> And the children of Benjamin gathered themselves together out of their cities unto Gibeah, to go out to battle against the children of Israel. And the children of Benjamin numbered on that day out of the cities twenty and six thousand men that drew sword ... besides seven hundred chosen men, were left-handed; every one could sling stones at a hair-breadth, and not miss.

But it seems that the rest of the Israelites also had considerable fighting ability: "And the men of Israel, numbered four hundred thousand men that drew sword; all these were men of war". Here, too, the coalition did not appreciate the opposing force, and it puts only one tribe against it, even though it was the best in fighting, the tribe of Judah-Yehuda, of course: "And the children of Israel arose, and went up to Beth-el, and asked counsel of God; and they said: 'Who shall go up for us first to battle against the children of Benjamin?' And the LORD said: 'Judah first.'" And the result is not long to come: "And the children of Benjamin came forth out of Gibeah, and destroyed down to the ground of the Israelites on that day twenty and two thousand men." And in their distress, the Israelites then: "And the children of Israel went up and wept before the LORD until even". Now the attacking coalition is acting more cautiously, and this time it is trying to successfully enlist the supreme fighting force to their aid: "Then all the children of Israel, and all the people, went up, and came unto Beth-el, and wept, and sat there before the LORD, and fasted that day until even; and they offered burnt-offerings and peace-offerings before the LORD". And after they pleased God, they succeed in the war, as this time the God stands on their side: "And the children of Israel asked of the LORD ... and Phinehas, the son of Eleazar, the son of Aaron [the Chief Priest], stood before it in those days—saying: 'Shall I yet again go out to battle against the children of Benjamin my brother, or shall I cease?' And the LORD said: 'Go up; for to-morrow I will deliver him into thy hand'".

And the fate of Benjamin, the fierce tribe from which the first king of Israel came [King Saul], was quite bitter this time ("Benjamin is a wolf that raveneth; in the morning he devoureth the prey, and at even he divideth the spoil") (Gen 49:27). Then, according to the verse, "And there fell of Benjamin eighteen thousand men; all these were men of valour". But this is still not the end of the defeat, the coalition ambushed the city and is now penetrating: "And the liers-in-wait hastened, and rushed upon Gibeah (Benjamin's major city); and the liers-in-wait drew forth, and smote all the city with the edge of the sword". And if that is not enough:

> [The] Benjamites looked behind them, and, behold, the whole of the city went up in smoke to heaven ... And they turned and fled toward the wilderness unto the rock of Rimmon; and they gleaned of them in the

> *highways five thousand men; and followed hard after them unto Gidom, and smote of them two thousand men. So that all who fell that day of Binyamin were twenty and five thousand men that drew the sword; all these were men of valour.*

And there was little left of Binyamin:

But six hundred men turned and fled toward the wilderness unto the rock of Rimmon; And the men of Israel turned back upon the children of Benjamin, and smote them with the edge of the sword, both the entire city, and the cattle, and all that they found; moreover all the cities which they found they set on fire, as the Romans said later in history—woe to the vanquished, indeed, a rather severe defeat.

However, this sad episode during the crystallization of the tribes of Israel also had a happy ending, and the magnificent tribe of Binyamin remained on the pages of history and even gained the privilege to provide the first king of Israel, King Saul. The rehabilitation process describes two different and interesting approaches of how women were found to the survivors of the battle. One is a warlike way—the misfortune of the residents of Jabesh-Gilead and their memory as those who did not join the coalition at that time came to their attention. Now they were called upon to pay the price, a heavy price as the Scripture tells:

> *And they said: 'What one is there of the tribes of Israel that came not up unto the LORD to Mizpah?' And, behold, there came none to the camp from Jabesh-gilead to the assembly ... and the congregation sent thither twelve thousand men of the valiantest, and commanded them, saying: 'Go and smite the inhabitants of Jabesh-gilead with the edge of the sword, with the women and the little ones ... and they found among the inhabitants of Jabesh-gilead four hundred young virgins, that had not known man by lying with him; and they brought them unto the camp to Shiloh, ... and the whole congregation sent and spoke to the children of Benjamin that were in the rock of*

> Rimmon, and proclaimed peace unto them . . . and they gave them the women whom they had saved alive of the women of Jabesh-gilead (Judg 21, 1-14).

However, it turns out that this solution was only partial. This time, surprisingly, they did not resort again to the sword but to more social means, and indeed the human imagination provided a solution of peace and admirable romance:

> And they said: 'Behold, there is the feast of the LORD from year to year in Shiloh, . . . And they commanded the children of Benjamin, saying: 'Go and lie in wait in the vineyards; . . . and see, and, behold, if the daughters of Shiloh come out to dance in the dances, then come ye out of the vineyards, and catch you every man his wife of the daughters of Shiloh, and go to the land of Benjamin . . . And the children of Benjamin did so, and took them wives, according to their number, of them that danced, whom they carried off; and they went and returned unto their inheritance, and built the cities, and dwelt in them (Judg 21, 19-23).

Indeed, a successful, peaceful solution.

It should be noted here that there are scholars who attribute this war to the struggle between the House of David and the House of Saul, primarily based on the story that Judah (the tribe of David) attacked first. Here, however, it might be difficult to explain the late appearance of the Kingdom of Judah (see below) and the joining of the tribe of Binyamin, the tribe of King Saul with their dominant leader Abner Ben-Ner, to the kingdom of Judah.

Occupation of the Land— History and Archeology

Historically, it is clear from archaeological evidence that Jericho was destroyed around 1550 BCE, long before the appearance of the group of Israelites, whereas Ai and Bethel

The Origin of the Hebrews and Their Faith

were not cities at all, but rather villages with relatively short periods of existence in the Late Bronze Age (1550–1200 BCE). The same is true for the results of the excavations at Giv'on.[5] As mentioned, the Torah and Joshua books describe personal and group conquests (such as Havat Yair in the Gilead region), which indeed indicate that there was no unified Israeli occupation. It is interesting to note that in the letters found in Tel el-Amarna, the capital of Egypt from the time of the Egyptian rule in Canaan (the middle of the second millennium BCE), there are complaints from the ruler of Shechem [שְׁכֶם—Shkhem] about the Habiru/Khabiru (Hebrews?). In findings from Ugarit in the north, they were also called A'piru, people who are not permanent residents, who try to take control of Shechem. See "And it came to pass . . . that . . . sons of Jacob . . . took each man his sword, and came upon the city (Shechem) unawares, and slew all the males" (Gen 34,25). And Jacob's own testimony when he is giving a privilege of inheritance to the two sons of Joseph: "Moreover I have given to thee one portion above thy brethren, which I took out of the hand of the Amorite with my sword and with my bow" (Gen 48, 22).

As for the appearance of the Israelites in the land of Canaan, as mentioned below, they are first mentioned in an Egyptian document from the beginning of the thirteenth century (circa 1207 BCE), in the victory stele (stone monument with engraved text) called "The Israel Stele" of Pharaoh Merneptah (1213–1203 BCE) (Figure III.1). This document describes a campaign of conquest in the land of Canaan, where Pharaoh mentions victory over city-states such as Ashkelon and Gezer and a tribal entity called Israel.

---

5. Isserlin, *The Israelites*, 57; Tubb, *Canaanites*.

Figure III.1: "The Israel Stele"; Line 27—"ysri₃r", I I I.

These people were in the center of the mountains or the Galilee,[6] but it is not clear when and how they arrived there. However, most scholars accept this period as the time of their appearance in the land of Canaan. They might have

---

6. Isserlin, *The Israelites*, 58–66; Tubb, *Canaanites*.

arrived earlier as wandering shepherds, and it took them time to adopt farming methods used in the land of Canaan in order to settle there.

Nevertheless, the archaeological findings do not support entry by an organized occupation as is told. Later, a clear relation to Israel as a kingdom is noted in Assyrian scriptures beginning in the ninth century BCE (see below).

Most scholars believe that the entity "Israel" formed as a result of a prolonged social process in the region, which also includes limited conquests by different groups. For example, it is interesting to note that immediately after the story of the organized war with Sihon the king of the Amorites and Og the king of Bashan,

> And the children of Machir the son of Manasseh went to Gilead, and took it, and dispossessed the Amorites that were therein ... and he dwelt therein. And Jair the son of Manasseh went and took the villages thereof, and called them Havvoth-jair. And Nobah went and took Kenath, and the villages thereof, and called it Nobah, after his own name (Num 32, 39-42).

As mentioned, immediately after the description of the well-organized war against the various 31 kings of Canaan (rulers of cities/states), the same military organization suddenly disappeared and was replaced by a description of individual tribes of Israel fighting separately against the inhabitants of the land, creating from time to time a narrow ad hoc coalition to fight against common enemy.

This description is concordant with archeological findings indicating that there was no unified occupation of the land. There was probably penetration, gradual expansion without war as well, and the joining of groups that had been expelled from other places, such as those who had fled from Egypt. Finally, the social process of forming a political entity includes the adoption of an original, new religion in this region.

The Settlement in the Land of Canaan

Archaeological findings indicate that towards the end of the thirteenth century BCE, there was a large increase in settlements with Israeli characteristics in the eastern part of the country, which were not there before. Israel Finkelstein suggests that the initial settlement was in the areas of the tribes of Ephraim and Menashe, where the nucleus of Israeli settlement was formed.[7] This may be appropriate for the story of Israeli infiltration and settlement in the east of the country, an area most suitable for grazing sheep: "Now the children of Reuben and the children of Gad had a very great multitude of cattle; and when they saw the land of Jazer, and the land of Gilead, that, behold, the place was a place for cattle" (Num 32, 1–5).

The assemblage of the tribes was gradual, and the alignment of the Twelve Tribes was probably created only shortly before the appearance of the monarchy with the joining of the southern tribe of Judah and its contribution to the war against the oppressive Philistines. As noted in the previous chapter, the story of the patriarchs and of the common origins of the tribes as descendants of one ancestor, Jacob who became Israel, are very much emphasized, probably as an ideological necessity for the purpose of crystalizing the tribes to a unified ethnic entity.

In conclusion, it can be seen that the conquest of the land of Canaan was much more difficult and complex than the relatively simplistic ideological description of a one-time occupation of the territory by an organized, fighting people. The description in the Book of Judges is undoubtedly more realistic about the chronicle of the struggles and difficulties of the tribes. This is as shown in this chapter and concordant with the Scripture itself: "In those days there was no king in Israel; every man did that which was right in his own eyes" (Judg 21, 25). This struggle with the inhabitants and between the tribes themselves persisted probably for hundreds of

---

7. Isserlin, *The Israelites*, 67.

years until the formation of the monarchy, under the enormous pressure of the Philistines.

The establishment of the kingdom: Israel and Judah

It is of special interest that the attempt to find objective support from archaeological and historical sources external to the biblical description of the beginning of the monarchy and the empire of David and Solomon encountered numerous difficulties. First, as mentioned, the name "Israel" appears for the first time only in the Victory Stele of Pharaoh Merneptah (1213-1203 BCE); this pharaoh embarked on a war campaign against the cities of the Land of Israel, such as Ashkelon and Gezer. In that context the name of Israel is mentioned; however as semi-nomadic people, but not as a unified entity as city or state. Israel as a political entity is mentioned only from the ninth century BCE as a nation state in the land of Canaan. At the same time, Aram, Edom, Moab, and other countries in the region were also formed.

In the description of the comprehensive campaign of war in the land of Canaan (924 BCE) by Pharaoh Shoshenq, mentioned in the Book of Kings as Pharaoh Shishak, which is documented on the wall of Amun temple in Karnak, Egypt, there is mention of only major city-states of the country, including Gaza, Beersheba, Arad, Ta'anach, and Beit Shean. However, Jerusalem is not mentioned at all as mentioned in the Book of Kings, and even the names Israel or Judah (Yehudah) are not.

> *And it came to pass in the fifth year of king Rehoboam, that Shishak king of Egypt came up against Jerusalem; and he took away the treasures of the house of the LORD, and the treasures of the king's house; he even took away all; and he took away all the shields of gold which Solomon had made (1 Kgs 14, 25-26).*

The Settlement in the Land of Canaan

Israel as a state is mentioned for the first time in the Victory Stele of Shalmaneser III of Assyria against a coalition of kings in the land of Canaan. The Battle of Qarqar in 853 BCE in the north of the country, is described in the Monolith of Kurkh (a village currently in the Turkish Kurdistan), "... 2000 chariots and 10,000 infantry of Ahab the Israelite (King Ahab)", a larger army than that of the other kings in the coalition.

In another document, the "Black Obelisk" (Figure III.2), the victory over the Kingdom of Israel is included with an engraving of the image of King Jehu, who reigns after Ahab, kneeling before Shalmaneser III (858–824 BCE) as a sign of surrender; however, that without mention of Judah.

Figure III.2: The Black Obelisk, showing King Jehu of Israel kneeling before the Assyrian king Shalmaneser III.

Israel is again mentioned in the stele of Mesha king of Moab, dated to 840 BCE, which removed the burden of the enslavement of "the son of Omri, king of Israel". Also, in a later historical document of the king of Assyria, Adir Nirari, who ruled in 810–783 BCE, his war against Israel and the Philistines in the south is described, but this without mention of Judah (which had to exist in the same region).

The Kingdom of Judah is mentioned only in documents from the eighth century BCE, about a century or more after the Kingdom of Israel, for the first time by Tiglath-pileser III, King of Assyria (745–727 BCE). King Ahaz of Jerusalem turned to Assyria for help against Israel. The campaign of war that followed caused almost the destruction of the Kingdom of Israel and weakened it most.[8]

The destruction of the kingdom of Israel came only a little later, in 722 BCE by Shalmaneser V (726–722 BCE), followed by Sargon (721–705 BCE):

> And it came to pass in the fourth year of king Hezekiah, which was the seventh year of Hoshea son of Elah king of Israel, that Shalmaneser king of Assyria came up against Samaria (the capital of the kingdom of Israel), and besieged it. And at the end of three years they took it; even in the sixth year of Hezekiah, which was the ninth year of Hoshea king of Israel, Samaria was taken. And the king of Assyria carried Israel away unto Assyria, and put them in Halah, and in Habor, on the river of Gozan, and in the cities of the Medes (2 Kgs 18, 9-11).

Thus, the overwhelming majority of the Israeli people (ten out of the twelve tribes) were dispersed, assimilated, and lost forever in less than 500 years after its inception.

The kingdom of Judah is mentioned later in the testimony of Sennacherib, King of Assyria (Tylor Prism, British Museum), describing the campaign of conquests in the region (691–689 BCE). It is important to note that the historical accuracy of the description in the Book of Kings is not fully compatible with this documentation. The siege on Jerusalem

---

8. Isserlin, *The Israelites*; Mitchell, *The Bible in the British Museum*; Tubb, *Canaanites*.

The Settlement in the Land of Canaan

mentioned in the Book of Kings including the miracle that occurred when the siege was suddenly removed is difficult to explain:

> Now in the fourteenth year of king Hezekiah did Sennacherib king of Assyria come up against all the fortified cities of Judah, and took them ... And the king of Assyria sent Tartan and Rab-saris and Rab-shakeh from Lachish to king Hezekiah with a great army unto Jerusalem. And they went up and came to Jerusalem (2 Kgs 18, 13-17).

Then, following the prayer of King Hezekiah, the scripture tells, the miraculous event happened:

> And it came to pass that night, that the angel of the LORD went forth, and smote in the camp of the Assyrians a hundred fourscore and five thousand; and when men arose early in the morning, behold, they were all dead corpses. So Sennacherib king of Assyria departed, and went and returned, and dwelt at Nineveh (2 Kgs 19, 35–36).

Sennacherib's story describes the capture of forty-six cities from Judah, taking many prisoners and very much looting, but is missing the description of the siege of Jerusalem. According to the Assyrian description, Hezekiah dealt with the fortification of Jerusalem, but when he saw Sennacherib's mighty power, he sent a delegation of dignitaries with a large ransom of money, gold, and valuables, all of which were taken to Nineveh the capital of Assyria.

The conquests of Sennacherib and the gift given to him—which is defined as tax—are indeed mentioned in the Book of Kings:

> And Hezekiah king of Judah sent to the king of Assyria to Lachish, saying: 'I have offended; return from me; that which thou puttest on me will I bear.' And the king of Assyria appointed unto Hezekiah king of Judah three hundred talents of silver and thirty talents of gold. And Hezekiah gave him all the silver

73

that was found in the house of the LORD, and in the treasures of the king's house (Kings II 18, 14–15).

In the decoration of a stone relief of an entire wall in his palace (now in the British Museum), the king of Assyria portrays his journey (701 BCE), in which he especially described the siege on the fortified city of Lachish, the conquest of it, and the exile of its inhabitants (Figure III.3), while Jerusalem is not mentioned. It appears therefore that the story in the Book of Kings ignoring the fate of the central city of Lachish and referring to the siege of Jerusalem was probably written a long time after the event itself without reliable historical documentation from that time, and apparently from a religious orientation to emphasize a miraculous occurrence for YHWH—an advocate king, Hezekiah.

The Settlement in the Land of Canaan

Figure III.3: The exile of the inhabitants of Lachish. Decoration from the palace of the Assyrian King Sennacherib in Nineveh.

As for the establishment of the United Kingdom by Kings David and Solomon, which was later divided into Israel and Judah, as written, it is interesting to note that there is no historical record or reference to such an Israeli empire. The names of David and Solomon are not mentioned in any document from that period, despite the wars and international relations described in the Book of Kings. In contrast to that, the kings of Israel appear and are well-documented, such as in the Black Obelisk of the Assyrian king mentioned above, in which King Jehu appears, and in the stele of Mesha king of Moab. In addition, of the two kingdoms only the Kingdom of Israel had a recognized international status. It seems, therefore, according to the scholars, that Judah separated from the kingdom of Israel, probably after the fall of the Omri dynasty.[9]

Archaeologically, it should be noted that the remains of magnificent buildings described in Jerusalem, especially in the context of King Solomon, were not found there, while they were found in Samaria, the capital of Israel, such as Ahab's ivory palace. Even the impressive stables that were attributed to Solomon in accordance with the writing were later found to correspond to the style found in Samaria and other fortified cities of Israel. The settlement of Ezion-Geber, over the Red Sea and with trade with Africa, was probably an Israeli initiative that was later attributed to Solomon, probably to award glory to the beginning of the Judean kingdom. It is interesting that, in the Bible, the kingdom of Israel is mentioned in relation to Ezion-Geber: "And after this did Jehoshaphat king of Judah join himself with Ahaziah king of Israel . . . to make ships to go to Tarshish; and they made the ships in Ezion-geber" (2 Chr 20, 35-36). The Aramaic style that appears in the sentence may indicate that it was composed after the Babylonian exile, and therefore the reference to Solomon in the Book of Kings is an anachronism.

---

9. Isserlin, *The Israelites*; Tubb, *Canaanites*.

The Settlement in the Land of Canaan

The only place where the name David might be mentioned is the "Tel Dan inscription" of the king of Aram, apparently Haza'el, indicating his victory over Jehoram son of Ahab, king of Israel, and possibly Ahaziah son of Jehoram king of Judah, probably referred to as the "King of the House of David", as it is written: "[I killed Jeho]ram son of [Ahab] king of Israel, and kil[led Ahaz]yahu the son of [Jehoram] kin[g] of Bidod/Bidud (ביתדוד)". The term Bitdod/Bitdud may be translated to בית דוד—Beit David (house of David), which should come in two separate words. The writing in brackets denotes additions by the scholars, among whom there are also those who believe that the expression ביתדוד indicates something other than Beit David—house of David.

It is interesting that the killing of these kings, who are well-mentioned in the Book of Kings, is attributed there to Jehu, which clearly attests to various sources or traditions that the Jewish writer (resident of Judah) had, a writer who was likely to have acted in later times.

Of course, it should be noted that this Aramaic certificate is from a later period in which the kingdom of Judah was already known and it is possible that the reference to the House of David is only an expression of the pedigree attribution, which was already established by the kings of Judah themselves. King Solomon, with all the numerous construction projects described and the family connection with Pharaoh, the king of Egypt, remains a mystery from historical and archaeological points of view.

As mentioned, the appearance of the Kingdom of Judah, only about a hundred years after the Kingdom of Israel, raises other theories as to its formation. In light of the objective findings, there are scholars who believe that David was a local tribal king as described in the Biblical sources. He began as a gang leader as explicitly stated in the Book of Samuel: "And every one that was in distress, and every one that was in debt, and every one that was discontented, gathered themselves unto him; and he became captain over them; and there were with him about four hundred men" (2 Sam 22, 2).

The collection of protection fees is well-described in the case of Nabal the Carmelite who apparently paid with his life for his refusal, as the text attributes a sudden death following this refusal: "And it came to pass about ten days after, that the LORD smote Nabal, so that he died" (1 Sam 25, 38). His wife Abigail was also taken even though the text apparently softens the event by bringing a surprising statement about her husband: "Let not my lord, I pray thee, regard this base fellow, even Nabal; for as his name is, so is he: Nabal is his name, and churlishness is with him" (1 Sam 25, 25). This is without mentioning in the entire story what wrong Nabal the Carmelite did.

It seems therefore that this might be a later tendentious story that emerged to beautify the image of David; apparently events of this kind and others were linked to his name, and also to enhance the importance of the Kingdom of Judah. This tendency appears clearly throughout David's biblical history, such as the harsh story of King Saul's rejection by Samuel the spiritual leader and the election of David in his place.

The grounds described for Saul's rejection seem minor, such as offering the sacrifice before Samuel's late arrival to the scene or looting sheep and cattle of the Amalekites by the people that were forbidden, as it is told by Samuel. Interestingly, the story of murdering the priests in the city of Nov by Saul is not mentioned as grounds for his rejection, which may attest to a later addition of that story.

At the end, the text mentions that David succeeded in being anointed as a king by Samuel the spiritual leader, according to the religious ceremony required for the legitimization of the ruler. This is even before David was mentioned as a captain of his own tribe Judah in Shechem for seven years before becoming king of Israel. This raises again

The Settlement in the Land of Canaan

the possibility of a later addition (an interesting comparison to the need for religious legitimacy, is the act of Napoleon Bonaparte in 1804 who made the Catholic Pope Pius VII come from Rome to his coronation ceremony as Emperor, where Napoleon put the crown on his own head).

It should be mentioned here that, seemingly, even the ethnic purity of David himself was also questioned. Therefore, there was apparently a need for writing the Book of Ruth, the story of Ruth the Moabite who accepted the yoke of the Lord YHWH and became a kosher Jewish woman by all accounts (even without the conversion process) who was married to the distinguished man Boaz. The most significant evidence of this tendentious story is the sudden transition at the end of the scroll from a narrative-descriptive story of a social nature to a quick, concise, and very purposeful conclusion—the bottom line: "... and Boaz begot Obed; and Obed begot Jesse, and Jesse begot David" (Ruth 4, 21–22).

Without a thorough study, it seems clear that David's story was written much later than the real time where even some elementary details were no longer fully known. The essential story of the rise of the name of David—the founder of the dynasty of Judah—in connection with the kingdom of the House of Saul appears in two different versions of the Book of Samuel. Moreover, even the famous battle with the mighty warrior Goliath the Philistine appears later in the book of Shmuel in a different version: "And there was again war with the Philistines at Gob; *and Elhanan the son of Jaare-oregim* the Beth-lehemite *slew Goliath the Gittite*, the staff of whose spear was like a weaver's beam" (2 Sam 21, 19). [Beth-lehemite is from Beith-Lehem or Bethlehem, the town of David's origin] This is as compared the description with David: "And there went out a champion from the camp of the Philistines, named Goliath of Gath ... And the shaft of his spear was like a weaver's beam" (1 Sam 17, 4–7). It follows from these descriptions that David's war with Goliath might be questionable. The interpretive form of the version with

David explaining who Goliath is and where he is from may be indicative of late writing that required further elaboration to the reader.

All of the biblical material clearly shows the tendency of the writer who probably served the royal house of Judah or the later editor after the exile when the temple was reestablished in Jerusalem, to beautify his name and to strengthen David's image and his kingdom as is proper for the founder of the dynasty. Nevertheless, the most striking is the gap between the image of David as described in the Book of Kings including the act with David's captain Uriah the Hittite whose wife Bathsheba he took and him he sent to death, and the religious-spiritual figure, full of justice, faith, and supplication attributed to him in Psalms. Such attributes that earned him the title "Na'im Zimrot Israel—נעים זמרות ישראל" [A kind singer of Israel or The sweet singer of Israel] (2 Sam 23, 1). Indeed, a spiritual figure such as this, along with political leadership, is the ideal figure for the Messiah to come.

In conclusion, this transformation in the image of David and the attribution of the great construction projects to Solomon, may be ascribed with great probability to the priests of the YHWH Temple in Jerusalem who served the Davidic dynasty and were therefore interested in its continuity and glory. These priests were the ones who edited the Torah scrolls in the days of Josiah (see chapter II) and probably also the religious historiography of the royal family, perhaps near or soon after the destruction of Jerusalem by Babylon.

It should be noted, however, that these documents were written from a religious point of view, and their appreciation for examples of the various kings who "did good in the sight of the LORD", or "did evil in the eyes of the LORD" are apparent. Great kings such as Omri, Ahab, and Jeroboam the son of Yoash, "who conquered Damascus and Hamath", with an international standing, are very faintly mentioned

The Settlement in the Land of Canaan

or even with hostile esteem. However, it should be kept in mind that even if these documents lack historical precision, they are still with us today thanks to the work of these clerics. This work that was imparted to Judaism, and later on to the religions that evolved from it or under its influence, the spiritual, moral, and trustworthy values today are common to many peoples.

In summary of the chapter on the formation of the entity Israel, it should be noted that all the historical documents and archaeological findings show that the organization of Israel as a socio-political entity began around the end of the thirteenth century BCE (late Bronze Era), when the Hittite empire collapsed and the Egyptian power withdrew from the region. This led to a commercial-economic retreat. Well-known cities ceased to exist and people began migrating to agricultural areas, including the mountainous region in the center of Canaan. These people were semi-nomadic, mainly sheep and cattle breeders, who subsequently became permanent rural residents, as can be seen from the description in Judges (farms of Yair in Gilead and others). Subsequently, there was a consolidation of groups in the region for state-social entities, forming city-states such as Shechem, Jericho, Gezer, and Megiddo. This was followed by the formation of political, state entities including Israel (early ninth century BCE), Aram, Edom, and later Assyria, which developed into a regional power, which together with Egypt later determined the fate of the entire region.

The consolidation of the tribes into a unified socio-political entity was gradual, as can be seen from the Book of Judges. For example, as noted that in the "Song of Deborah" (Judg 5) most prominent is the absence of the mighty tribe of Judah-Yehuda from the list of fighting tribes, probably as evidence that the southern tribe associated with the Moabites was not yet integrated into the evolving Israeli coalition. This was completed only under the immense pressure of the Philistines. Another example is the joining of the tribe of Dan, who settled in the Sidonian city of Laish, re-named Dan, and apparently engaged in sea trade as the Sidonians themselves did, as evidenced by the verse "and Dan, why doth he sojourn by the ships? who dwelt at the shore of the sea, and abideth by its bays" (Song of Deborah, Book of Judges, 5). And in another place "Dan shall judge his people, as one of the tribes of Israel" (Genesis 49, 16). These verses can allude to the joining of Dan, which is close to Sidon, as "one of the tribes of Israel" that existed then.

The family bond with the northern Canaanite peoples was also described, such as the copper artist who made the copper pillars in Solomon's Temple:

> *And King Solomon sent and fetched Hiram out of Tyre. He was the son of a widow of the tribe of Naphtali, and his father was a man of Tyre, a worker in brass . . . and he came to King Solomon and wrought all his work. Thus he fashioned the two pillars of brass (1 Kgs 7, 13–15).*

And, of course, "King Solomon loved many foreign women, besides the daughter of Pharaoh, women of the Moabites, Ammonites, Edomites, Zidonians, and Hittites" (1 Kgs 11, 1). And his son, who reigned after him, Rehoboam [רְחַבְעָם—Rehavam], is the son of Na'ama the Ammonite, and another famous example of the infamous Queen of Israel, Isabelle/Jesebel [איזבל—Izebel, Hebrew: pile of trash] the Sidonite, the wife of king Ahab.

The expansion of the Philistines (1080-900 BCE) and their pressure on the tribes of the region were the glue that eventually united the separate tribes into a unified political body from which the Kingdom of Israel emerged in the tenth-ninth century BCE. The historiosophy required by this national union includes the establishment of a common ancestral origin and the adaptation of an exclusive God, יְהוָה—YHWH, as discussed earlier (see chapter II).

The next chapter will discuss the theology—God's Law and the social ethics of Moses and its sources. Theology and morality—"that I am the LORD who exercise *mercy, justice,* and *righteousness,* in the earth; for in these things I delight, saith the LORD" (Jer 9, 23) that became the heritage of the Jewish people throughout the generations and which was later inherited by the entire Western society.

Chapter IV

Moses and the Hebrew Theology

The man Moses

AS PREVIOUSLY INDICATED, THE central figure responsible for the Hebrew theology and moral code, to whom attributed the establishment of the Hebrew people themselves as a unique social entity—is the man Moses. What are the sources of the Torah (teaching—Law) of Moses, as it is called in the tradition [ספר תורת משה—Sefer Torat Moshe, Teaching book or Teaching Law of Moses] (Josh 8, 31; Josh 23, 6; 2 Kgs 14, 6; 2 Chr 34, 14; Neh 8, 1).

In contrast to the patriarchs, whose connection with Aram and Mesopotamia is emphasized, the connection between Moshe and Egypt and the Midianites is dominant. As mentioned, this connection is probably of the utmost importance to the origin of Moses' theology.

In the description of God's revelation, remarkable is the dialogue that took place between Moses and God, a dialogue that hints at the new theology. This dialogue presents some important key points; one is the uncertainties of Moshe as how to present the god who revealed to him to the society that he chose:

Moses and the Hebrew Theology

> And Moses said unto God: 'Behold, when I come unto the children of Israel, and shall say unto them: The God of your fathers hath sent me unto you; and they shall say to me: What is His name? what shall I say unto them?' (Exod 3, 13).

A second point is the theological representation of God. God explicitly indicates his name:

> And God said moreover unto Moses: 'Thus shalt thou say unto the children of Israel: יהוה—YHWH, the God of your fathers, the God of Abraham, the God of Isaac, and the God of Jacob, hath sent me unto you; this is My name for ever, and this is My memorial unto all generations (Exod 3, 15).

But it is very surprising and of primary significance that this name is new, a name that was not known before to the forefathers of the chosen people: "And God spoke unto Moses and said unto him: 'I am the LORD; and I appeared unto Abraham, unto Isaac, and unto Jacob, as God Almighty [אֵל שַׁדָּי—El Shadai], *but by My name*יהוה*—YHWH I made Me not known to them*" (Exod 6, 2-3). Thus, this statement is clearly indicating a new divine entity.

Indeed, this recognition between אֵל שַׁדָּי—El Shadai/ El Almighty and יהוה—YHWH seems to emerge after the appearance of Moses and Aaron before the Children of Israel and then before Pharaoh (Exodus Chapter 3 El Shadai; YHWH—Exodus Chapter 6). It is possible that only after the first encounter does this association come to Moshe, and only then does he attribute his God to the ancient God of the Hebrews. In summary, it is quite clear from the text that the God that Moses presents to the Hebrews, YHWH is not the same God who was revealed to the believers in the land of Canaan—El Shadai—God Almighty. This God has new characteristics, attributes that have long existed in the Egyptian faith. The God who was, who is, and who will be [הייה, הווה, יהייה], which contain the basic characters: י—Y, ה—H,ו—W, ה—H; יהוה—YHWH, and therefore it is important to emphasize this fundamental characteristic in his name "YHWH". He is no longer the god of a family or a city as was the custom in the past, like El-Beith'el, but He is a cosmic, universal "god", he is Elohim—אֱלֹהִים plural of El-god, that exists forever, and therefore is henceforth entitled to the new name "יהוה—YHWH". Compare to the ancient Egyptian text "He has existed forever and ever, and he will be forever", as detailed below.

The Egyptian theology and the monotheism of Moses

A study of the principles of the ancient Egyptian faith that existed for more than a thousand years before the time described in the scripture for the appearance of Moses, strongly suggest the theological origin of the Torah's teachings and beyond, as will be presented here.[1]

God Oneness

The following Egyptian text (in *italics*) is taken from the papyri that have been preserved in graves for more than 5,000 years, and are displayed for inspection at the British Museum in London.[2] *"God is One, alone and none other existeth"*. Compare to the Biblical text: "Hear, O Israel: the LORD our God, the LORD is One" (Deut 6, 4) and "that I, even I, am He, and there is no god with Me" (Deut 32, 39).

God eternal and infinite

"God is from the beginning... God is the eternal, He is eternal and infinite; and endureth for ever ... He shall endure to all

---

1. See Isserlin, *The Israelites*; Tubb, *Canaanites*; Wallis Budge, *Egyptian Ideas of the Afterlife*, 18–23.
2. Wallis Budge, *Egyptian Ideas of the Afterlife*.

eternity"; compare to: The God who was, is and will be (הייה הווה, יהייה), and

> And God said moreover unto Moses: 'Thus shalt thou say unto the children of Israel: The LORD YHWH—יְהוָה ... hath sent me unto you; this is My name for ever... (Exodus 3, 15); Ye are My witnesses, saith the LORD, and My servant whom I have chosen; that ye may know and believe Me, and understand that I am He; before Me there was no God formed, neither shall any be after Me (Isa 43, 10).

And the well-established prayer "Adon Olam—"אדון עולם: "The Lord of universe who reigned before all creation is created, and He was, and He is, and He shall endure for glory. And after all existing things are ended; alone he will reign awe-inspiring, without beginning and without ending..."

The transcendental God

"He cannot be figured in stone; he is not to be seen in a sculptured image ..."; *"thou canst not conceive his form in thy heart"*; Compare to "Thou shalt not make unto thee a graven image, nor any manner of likeness, of anything that is in heaven above, or that is in the earth beneath, or that is in the water under the earth" (Exod 20, 3).

"No man hath known His form, No man hath been able to seek out His likeness"; Compare to Maimonides, the Jewish philosopher (1135–1204): "That He has no body, and that He cannot be attained by those in body, and He has no resemblance at all" (to any figure or an attribute) (*The Guide to the Perplexed*).

"The place where he lives is unknown; he is not to be found in inscribed shrine; there existeth no habitation which can contain him", Compare to: "But will God in very truth dwell on the earth? behold, heaven and the heaven of heavens cannot contain Thee; how much less this house ... !" (1 Kgs 8, 27); and "Thus saith the LORD: "... where is the house that ye

may build unto Me? And where is the place that may be My resting-place?" (Ezek 66, 1); and "I heard (the angels saying) . . . : 'Blessed be the glory of the LORD from His place'" (i.e., wherever he is) (Ezek 3, 12).

God the Creator

Here, too, the similarity to the Egyptian text is rather astonishing.

"*God Himself is existence*", "*God hath made the universe, and He hath created all that therein is*", "*He is the Creator of the heavens and the earth*", "*God has stretched out the heavens and founded earth*"; Compare to the biblical text in the Book of Genesis: "And God made the firmament, and divided the waters which were under the firmament from the waters which were above the firmament" (Gen 1, 7); and elsewhere, "Who made heaven and earth, the sea, and all that in them is" (Ps 146, 6); "I, even I, have made the earth, and created man upon it; I, even My hands, have stretched out the heavens, and all their host have I commanded" (Isa 45, 12).

"*The heaven rest upon Him and the earth under His feet*"; Compare to: "Thus saith the LORD: The heaven is My throne, and the earth is My footstool" (Isa 8, 1).

"*Who weigh heaven and earth in the balance*"; Compare to: "Who . . . meted out heaven with the span, and comprehended the dust of the earth in a measure, and weighed the mountains in scales, and the hills in a balance?" (Isa 40, 12).

"*He is the Primeval Potter, . . . He formed men . . . upon potter's table*", "*He giveth life to men, and He breatheth the breath of life into his nostrils*". Compare to: "Then the LORD God formed man of the dust of the ground, and breathed into his nostrils the breath of life; and man became a living soul" (Gen 2, 7).

"*He had spoken, His word came to pass, and it shall endure forever*"; Compare to: "For He spoke, and it was; He commanded, and it stood" (Ps 33,9).

"Amen", The ancient god

In comparing the Egyptian with the Israeli theology, it is very interesting to try finding the source and the meaning of the word "Amen" recited in daily prayers, as a declaration of affirmation—"so it will be", at the end of many prayers and in Biblical texts glorifying the God, very common in the book of Psalms. Amen is a major Egyptian god from the most ancient period—beginning in the prehistoric period (about 6000 years). Like the prefix of Hebrew names Yeho—יהו, part of YHWH [יְהוָה] names: Yehonatan, Yehoyada, Yehoyachin, Yehoshafat; and other theophoric names, the name Amen appears at the beginning of the names of many Egyptian kings: Amenhotep I to IV, Amennemhet I to IV, Amenmesse, and more.

God—the divine Ethics

"God is truth, and He liveth by truth", "He executeth truth throughout the entire world"; Compare to: "the LORD God is the truth" (Jer 10,10); "Righteousness and justice are the foundation of Thy throne; mercy and truth go before Thee" (Ps 89, 15); "Thy right hand is full of righteousness" (Ps 48, 11); "He loveth righteousness and justice" (Ps 33,5); "The LORD is righteous in all His ways, and gracious in all His works" (Ps 145,17); and "... I am the LORD who exercise mercy, justice, and righteousness, in the earth; for in these things I delight, saith the LORD" (Jer 9, 23).

"God is merciful unto those who reverence Him and He heareth him that calleth upon Him", "God knoweth him that serveth Him"; Compare to: "God, merciful and gracious, long-suffering, and abundant in goodness and truth" (Exod, 34,6); "The LORD is gracious, and full of compassion; slow to anger, and of great mercy. The LORD is good to all; and His tender mercies are over all His works" (Psalms 145, 8-9).

"The LORD is nigh unto all them that call upon Him, to all that call upon Him in truth. He will fulfil the desire of them that fear Him; He also will hear their cry, and will save them. The LORD preserveth all them that love Him" (Psalms 145, 18-20).

"He protecteth the weak against the strong", "He heareth the cry of him who is bound in fetters", "He judgeth between the mighty and the weak"; Compare to: Who executeth justice for the oppressed; who giveth bread to the hungry. The LORD looseth the prisoners; The LORD openeth the eyes of the blind; the LORD raiseth up them that are bowed down; the LORD loveth the righteous; The LORD preserveth the strangers; He upholdeth the fatherless and the widow (Ps 146, 7-9).

The social ethics— the Hebrew and Egyptian codex

It is of great interest to compare the moral-social code, as it appears in the Ten Commandments and later in the section Mishpatim—מִשְׁפָּטִים Statutes, in Exodus (chapter 21), and other books of the Torah, with the moral code of ancient Egypt. In the courtroom in front of the Egyptian gods, headed by Osiris, god of the afterlife and resurrection, the deceased confesses his sins (Figure IV.1; for an explanation see the Appendix). This confession has a structured formula, usually contains about 42 statements, all of which are formulated in a negative style; that is, all the negative acts that the deceased was careful not to do in his life.

Moses and the Hebrew Theology

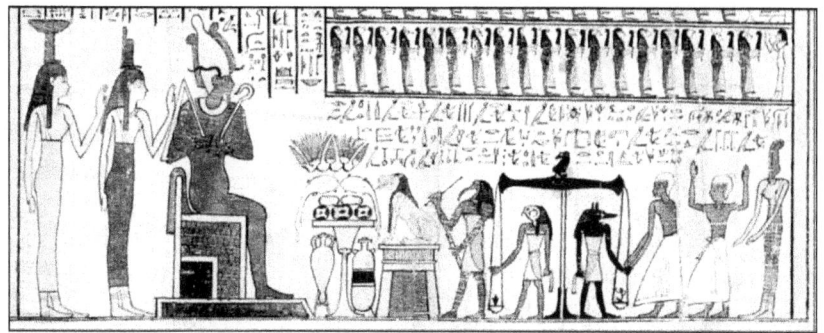

Figure IV.1: The divine judgement in ancient Egypt.

This confession includes statements that: *He did not commit murder, he did not commit theft, he did not commit adultery, he did not answer false testimony, he did not bear God's name in vain, he did not disrespect God, King, and man.*

It seems almost unnecessary to provide the reader with the text from the Ten Commandments and elsewhere in the Torah; for example: Thou shalt not murder. Thou shalt not commit adultery. Thou shalt not steal. Thou shalt not bear false witness against thy neighbour. Thou shalt not covet thy neighbour's house; thou shalt not covet thy neighbour's wife, nor his man-servant, nor his maid-servant, nor his ox, nor his ass, nor any thing that is thy neighbour's (Exod 20, 12-13). "... neither shall ye deal falsely, nor lie one to another" (Lev 19, 11). "Thou shalt not take the name of the LORD thy God in vain" (Exod 20, 6).

Other moral and imperative codes prevailed in the ancient Egypt society showing an astonishing resemblance to that in the Torah, following the Ten Commandments, and later on in the writings of the prophets. Here are some examples:

The Egyptian deceased continues his moral confession saying that he:

> *had not done evil, did not robe, he had not cheat in measures of volume, size and weight, did not deceive;*

> he had not act violently, and did not go with a group of wicked people. He had not done adultery. He was not dishonest or hypocritical; he had not done iniquity and did not discriminate between people. He had not acted deceitfully, had not utter falsehood and he listened to the words of justice and truth.

Later, there are other social-behavioral codes, such as avoiding rage and anger.

Compare to the Hebrew text:

> Thou shalt not wrest the judgment of thy poor in his cause. Keep thee far from a false matter; and the innocent and righteous slay thou not; for I will not justify the wicked. And thou shalt take no bribe; for a bribe blindeth them that have sight, and perverteth the words of the righteous (Exod 23, 6-8).

> Ye shall do no unrighteousness in judgment; thou shalt not respect the person of the poor, nor favour the person of the mighty; but in righteousness shalt thou judge thy neighbour (Lev 19, 15).

> Ye shall not steal; neither shall ye deal falsely, nor lie one to another (Lev 19, 11).

> Thou shalt not oppress thy neighbour, nor rob him (Lev 19, 16).

> Thou shalt not go up and down as a talebearer among thy people (Lev 19, 16).

> Thou shalt not take vengeance, nor bear any grudge against your fellow men; Thou shalt love thy neighbour as thyself: I am the LORD (Lev 19, 18).

> Ye shall do no unrighteousness in judgment, in meteyard, in weight, or in measure. Just balances, just weights, a just ephah (dry volume), and a just hin (liquid volume), shall ye have: I am the LORD your God, who brought you out of the land of Egypt (Lev 19, 35-36).

The final sentence is of special interest. The God who commands all of these statutes is the God who brought the people out of the land of Egypt, the land where these laws and statutes have been prevalent from time immemorial.

In summary, it seems quite clear that the moral imperative in ancient Egypt was very extensive and included a deep social behavioral awareness, which has not been achieved even to date in many societies despite the many moral doctrines that have since been established. It should be noted that in the Mesopotamian culture that developed at the same time, no such extensive moral system was found, and even the concept of justice in its abstract form did not seem to exist.[3]

For the reader who may still be hesitating to appreciate these relations between ancient Egyptian and Hebrew theology, here is a figure of a great interest. The Egyptian boys who are candidates for the priesthood are circumcised with a flint knife. Compare that with the story of Zipporah, Moses' wife: "Then Zipporah took a flint, and cut off the foreskin of her son" (Figure IV.2; Exod 4, 25). Perhaps this might be the meaning of the verse, "and ye shall be unto Me a kingdom of priests, and a holy nation" (Exod 19, 6).

---

3 Black and Green, *Gods, Demons and Symbols*.

The Origin of the Hebrews and Their Faith

Figure IV.2: Circumcision in ancient Egypt—
using a flint knife as described for Zipporah, the wife of Moses.

Summary of the chapter

From all the material presented, it may be concluded that the origin of the Hebrew people is of the tribes who lived in the region of Canaan, some of which, as is told about the forefathers, wandered from Aram (north to Israel). The influence of Mesopotamian, Sumerian, and Akkadian cultures is well-documented as evidenced in the Book of Genesis and other ancient writings, such as the Book of Job. It is interesting that the local culture already had a tendency toward monotheism, as is well implied in the words of the King of Shalem [Salem] (Jerusalem in the future—the city of the Canaanite God Shalem) to Abraham: "And Melchizedek king of Shalem [Salem] brought forth bread and wine; and he was priest of God the Most High. And he blessed him, and said: 'Blessed be Abram to God Most High, Maker of heaven and earth'" (Gen 18, 14).

At a later stage, however, this belief received a very definite theological character, where it deepened both the faith in an abstract god with no title and imagination at all, and the broad moral imperative derived from him, an indisputable divine decree. As shown above, this theology with its extensive moral injunctions is based, at least in part, on the ancient Egyptian theology.

The idea of monotheism, which apparently did not succeed in taking root in Egypt itself, was adapted and applied to a group of Semitic people. This purification of the Hebrew theology from any contamination of idolatry, except for the sacrificial work, identical to what was customary among the nations. See Maimonides' (Ha-Rambam) commentary on the Virtues of Mitzvot, saying that sacrificial work was a kind of an immature way to worshiping God, since it was practiced by all nations around and was viewed by the Hebrews as a customary way of worship (*Guide for the Perplexed*, Part Three, Chapter 32). Thus, it seems that the faith had undergone sublimation before being presented to the people from the East. It seems necessary therefore that there was a theological body that took its foundation from ancient Egypt, but selected the grain from the chaff and chose the refined part to place before the body that would constitute the sacred, model society:

> *Observe therefore and do them; for this is your wisdom and your understanding in the sight of the peoples, that, when they hear all these statutes, shall say: 'Surely this great nation is a wise and understanding people'* (Deut 4, 6).

Chapter V

The Development and Sublimation of the Jewish Monotheism

THE JEWISH MONOTHEISM INCLUDES two main elements: one, known and apparent to all, is the existence of a single God, which is the essence of the faith in the uniqueness and Oneness of God ("the LORD is one"). The second, which is often overlooked even by scholars, is that the One God is entirely abstract (as summarized by Maimonides, "He has no body . . . and has no imagination at all"). The Israelis did not choose one god from a vast pantheon of gods while continuing the idolatry of an anthropomorphic figure, but transformed God into a transcendent spirit that has no image, a symbol that can only be contemplated in mind but cannot be likened to anything in the human realm or even in an abstract attribute (interestingly that following this idea, the Jewish sages concluded thereafter that even "God, merciful and gracious, long-suffering, and abundant in goodness and truth" (Exod 34, 6) shouldn't have been written if it hadn't been uttered by Moses himself). It may be said that of these two elements, this is the more difficult to attain spiritually, and thus it expresses the unique contribution of Jewish faith to the sublimation of human theological thinking.

The Development of Jewish Monotheism

Islam was well able to emulate this abstraction, but it is quite of interest that the only religion that emerged directly from Judaism, Christianity, in its Helenistic-Roman transformation did not adopt this challenge and reserved to anthropomorphism of god. God himself was personified and humanized; to him an assembly of human figures was assigned as family members, such as the Holy Mother, Saint Joseph, Saint John the Baptist and Saint Elizabeth his mother. This anthropomorphism was probably necessary for the purpose of a visual ritual which, together with the abolition of the commandments of the Torah[1] by St. Paul [the Jewish-Roman Saul of Tarsus—שאול התרסי], facilitated the dissemination of the new faith among the pagan, peoples who needed simple theology and concrete figures as the object of their faith.

The two fundamental components of the Jewish monotheism are well presented in the first of the Ten Commandments, "I am the LORD thy God, ... Thou shalt have no other gods before Me" (Exod 20, 2). This is the first component of the singularity, and later came the second element of abstraction, "Thou shalt not make unto thee a graven image, nor any manner of likeness, of anything that is in heaven

---

1. Torah (Hebrew: teaching, Law) *Pentateuch*, is the first five books of the Hebrew Bible containing the teaching of God's law and statutes given by Moses. It is of interest that according to the New Testament (a term adopted from the Hebrew Bible, "Behold, the days come, saith the LORD, that I will make a new testament with the house of Israel, and with the house of Judah" (Jer 31, 30), there was no intent to withdraw from that teaching "Do not think that I have come to abolish the Law/Torah . . ." (Matt 5, 17). However, the Church doctrine holds the principle of *Sola fide* (faith alone), indicating that salvation comes through faith alone.

It might be of interest to the reader that the term New Testament was found again in the text of the Dead Sea cult writing "Serekh Hayakhad" (scroll 1QS), related maybe to the Essenes (Greek, Essenoi or Essaio; Hebrew איסיים). The cult lived approximately between 150BCE to 70 AD, time of destruction of Jerusalem by the Romans. They held strong Messianic belief and lived a monastic life with great importance given to baptism.

above, or that is in the earth beneath, or that is in the water under the earth" (Exod 20, 3).

It is conceivable that these two components did not develop simultaneously. The first appears to be a relatively rapid penetration, while the second is a gradual and evolutionary process. It is of significance that not only Abraham believed in a single supreme God, but also, as the script testifies, the king of Shalem/Salem, "and he was priest of God the Most High ... Maker of heaven and earth" (Gen 18, 14).

Of high interest is the fact is that the ancient Canaanite god, El—אֵל, is the same god who revealed himself to the forefathers, the patriarchs, in this title, though in several variations, such as El-Shadai, El-Elyon, or El-Beth-El. Nearby places, including Beth-El, are known for bearing the name of local gods with sacred stones where gods reside.[2] This finding surprisingly matches the biblical text: "And Jacob rose up early in the morning, and took the stone that he had put under his head, and set it up for a pillar, and poured oil upon the top of it and he called the name of that place Beth-El [Hebrew: literately, house of god]" (Gen 28, 18–19); and subsequently "And he built there an altar, and called the place El-Beth-El [Hebrew: god of Beth-El], because there God was revealed unto him" (Gen 35, 7).

The theophoric element "El" is intertwined with many personal names, such as Asael, Ezekiel, and of course the name Israel itself (IsraEl—the god who governs; "Sar"— Ruler in the ancient Akkadian language). This name is also used as first name in Ugarit and Ebla in the north in the early Bronze Age, the region of Aram from where the forefathers came, and indeed the names of the gods "El-Shadai" and "El-Elyon" are also mentioned there. This is together with the names Abram (as in the bible before it was transformed into Abraham), Ya'akov—Jacob, and Bilha—wife of Jacob, which appear in the writings from these regions.[3]

---

2. Isserlin, *The Israelites*, 259.

3. See also Sivan, *Ugaritic Grammar*.

The adoption of the newly chosen God, YHWH—יְהֹוָה, by the emerging people is revolutionary in its nature, for as has been mentioned, YHWH was not known and was not worshiped by the inhabitants of Canaan and the North until after the appearance of the Israelites in the region. However, from the Scriptures related to the First Temple (of Solomon) era, and from the books of the Prophets it is quite clear that despite the acceptance of YHWH as exclusive to the Israelites (see above), they have never ceased to serve the gods of the region, especially Ba'al and Asherah (Astrat, Ashtoret).

It is interesting that the union of "El" with "Astrate" was also adopted for the new Hebrew God; this is according to the archeological findings of inscriptions from the early royal period in Khirbet el-Qom near Hebron (ninth century BCE), in which there is a blessing in the name of YHWH and his consort Asherah (Figure V.1). In another inscription between the ninth and eighth centuries BCE (850–750) from Kuntillet-Ajrud in the region of the Kingdom of Israel in Sinai peninsula, there is a blessing in the name of YHWH of Samaria and his consort Asherah.

The Origin of the Hebrews and Their Faith

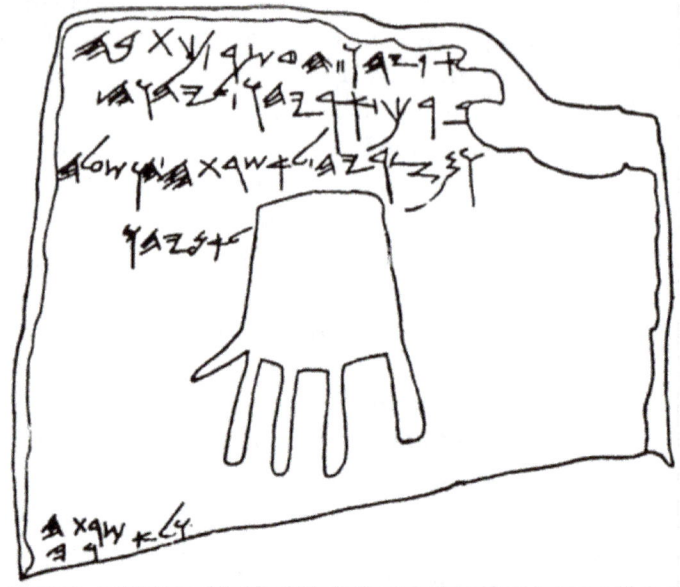

Figure V.1: A blessing in the name of YHWH and his consort Asherah (ninth century BCE).

Indeed, the scripture indicates that a statue of Ashera stood in the Lord's temple for extended periods, usually together with Ba'al, such as the case of Menasheh, son of Hezekiah king of Judah:

> For he built again the high places which Hezekiah his father had destroyed; and he reared up altars for Baal, and made an Asherah, as did Ahab king of Israel, and worshipped all the host of heaven, and served them . . . and built altars in the two courts of the house of the LORD (2 Kgs 21, 3-5).

Two generations later, king Josiah instituted a reform to restore the faith in YHWH:

> And the king commanded Hilkiah the high priest . . . to bring forth out of the temple of the LORD all the vessels that were made for Baal, and for the Asherah, and for all the host of heaven; and he burned them

> *without Jerusalem in the fields of Kidron, and carried the ashes of them unto Beth-el. And he put down the idolatrous priests ... that offered unto Baal, to the sun, and to the moon, and to the constellations, and to all the host of heaven. And he brought out the Asherah from the house of the LORD ... and he broke down the houses of the sodomites, that were in the house of the LORD, where the women wove coverings for the Asherah (2 Kgs 23, 4-7).*

The archeological findings from Jerusalem in the period of the kings of Judah also attest to the distribution of the idol worship. Remains of the ancient Canaanite fertility goddess Ashtoret/Astrat (Ashera), widespread throughout the Middle East at that time, were found in the largest numbers, hundreds in number, in excavations of houses in Jerusalem. The complete sculpture shown in Figure V.2 is from a tomb at the same period of time.[4]

---

4. Tubb, *Canaanites*.

Figure V.2: Asherah statue found in houses in Jerusalem—
Kingdom of Judah (900-586 BC).

These findings appear to be consistent with the testimony of the survivors of the destruction of Jerusalem themselves in the book of the prophet Jeremiah, confirming this reality.

> *Then all the men ... and all the women that stood by, a great assembly ... answered Jeremiah, saying: 'As for the word that thou hast spoken unto us in the name of the LORD (YHWH), we will not hearken*

> unto thee. But we will certainly perform every word that is gone forth out of our mouth, to offer unto the queen of heaven, and to pour out drink-offerings unto her, as we have done, we and our fathers, our kings and our princes, in the cities of Judah, and in the streets of Jerusalem'.

And, indeed, interesting is their justification, attesting to a crisis in the faith in God, "... for then had we plenty of food, and were well, and saw no evil. But since we let off to offer to the queen of heaven, and to pour out drink-offerings unto her, we have wanted all things, and have been consumed by the sword and by the famine" (Jer 44, 15-18).

It may be realized, therefore, that in general, the Israelite religion, from the beginning to the destruction of the First Temple (Solomon's Temple, 586 BC) was similar to the Canaanite and even depends on its models, especially in the practice of worship.[5] Similarity also exists with other neighboring regions, but this is of secondary importance. Such a similarity, for example, is the brass serpent found in the temple of the Midianites at Timna Springs in Israel, similar to the brass serpent "Nehushtan" [Nahash—נָחָשׁ, Snake] that was located in the Tabernacle and later in the Temple in Jerusalem. However, it is interesting to note that the Canaanite practice in the Late Bronze Age to create metal idols ceased immediately after the establishment of the Israelites; especially noteworthy is that there was no image attributed to YHWH.

Likewise, during the monarchy, the cult places that were so common up to the destruction of the Temple, were not decorated with Canaanite motifs such as a lion, a sphinx, or other idolatrous figure. It seems therefore that the Israelite religion tended to develop in its own direction, until it finally became very different from that of the surrounding peoples.

---

5. Darshan and Darshan, *Canaanite Mythology*; Isserlin, *The Israelites*, 260; Tubb, *Canaanites*.

The Origin of the Hebrews and Their Faith

In conclusion, it should be noted that although generally the faith in YHWH was indeed accepted and practiced within all the Israelite tribes (as mentioned in the Stele of Mesha king of Moab, 840 BCE, who fought the kingdom of Israel, "and I took ... the vessels of YHWH"), it flourished and became the main faith in the kingdom of Judea alone. This is probably due to the construction of the main temple of YHWH in Jerusalem, the influence of the priests, and the prophets of God, most of whom came from Jerusalem and Judea.

Towards the end of the First Temple, around the seventh and sixth centuries BCE, YHWH, despite the extensive worship of idolatry, became the most acceptable god to the inhabitants of Judah. This can be judged at least from the names of people, functionaries, and scribes from Judea mentioned in the Bible and found in many stamps recovered from that period. Most of these names contain the suffix "YAH": Zedekiah, Isaiah, Yazaniah, Jeremiah, Obadiah; or the prefix "YH": Yehonatan, Yehoyada, Yehoyachin, and more.[6] In addition, the title "Servant of Lord—YHWH—יְהוָה" was also found in a seal from the ninth century BCE. Only a small part of the seals contains components from the names of the surrounding gods. It is conceivable, however, that some of these seals may indeed belong to subjects of other origins, such as Hittit, Yebusit, Ammonit, and Sidonit, who were mixed within the Hebrew population. Not a few Hebrew princes and kings were born, for example, to foreign mothers, such as King Rehoboam who was the son of King Solomon and Queen Na'ama the Ammonite.

Additionally, in the Letters of Lachish—a major fortified town in Judah—that were found from that period, near the destruction of Jerusalem by the Babylonians (587 BCE), prevalent is the opening welcome in the name of the Lord—YHWH, "May YHWH bless you", or "May YHWH cause my

---

6. Isserlin, *The Israelites*, 258.

lord to hear tidings of peace", or "Shall YHWH show my lord
... peace", or such an oath "As YHWH lives..."[7]

In this context, it seems that the preservation of the sacred writings by the priests of the Lord in Jerusalem provided the basis for the renewal of the faith and the national entity in the Second Temple period (516 BCE to 70 CE) after the Babylonian exile, and hence the foundation of the Jewish faith and culture, which became the dominant characteristics of Judaism along the two thousand years of exile.

From a theological point of view, the ultimate exclusiveness of YHWH worship appeared only in the days of the Second Temple, where despite the overwhelming Hellenistic-Roman influence, paganism ceased to be a challenge of faith. However, the evolutionary process of God's abstraction continued, a process which demanded a great spiritual effort from the Jewish people. Although sacrifice continued to be practiced in the days of the Second Temple, it is most striking that the most sacred chamber of the Temple itself, the Holy of Holies [קודש הקודשים], which only the High Priest can enter, and this is only once a year on Yom Kippur after purification and baptism, did not contain The Ark of Covenant [אֲרוֹן הַבְּרִית]. The ark that hosts the stone Tablets of Covenant with the inscription of the Ten Commandments, and the golden statues of the winged Cherubs present in the first temple [Kerubim—[כְּרוּבִים]. These objects were never found after the Babylonian exile, a fact that was known to all; however, without an impact on the faith.

It is likely that this actuality was of a great surprise to the Roman commander Pompey, who came to Jerusalem—resulting later in the annexation of the Land of Israel as a colony in the Roman Empire (63 BCE). Pompey entered the Temple and even the Holy of Holies without finding anything tangible as the object of the Jewish people's faith.

---

7. The British Museum; Isserlin, *The Israelites*, 259.

Ironically, the ultimate abstraction of the faith came after the destruction of the Temple itself, for only then did the Jewish people disconnect from the pagan sacrifice practice that had existed in the region for thousands of years, turning it into a spiritual act of prayer alone (although there is evidence that prayers had already begun in the later days of the Second Temple).

It seems that even during the generations of the Jewish people in exile, the wall for pure spiritual monotheism required considerable reinforcement. The highest contribution to the sublimation of faith came not by chance from the greatest of the philosophers and thinkers who arose to the Jewish people, Maimonides; Moses, son of Maimon [Ha-Rambam—הרמב"ם], "From Moses to Moses there were none like Moses".

With a powerful ability of Halakhic knowledge (Jewish Law), high philosophical capacity, and a rare analytical facility, Maimonides, in his book *The Guide for the Perplexed*, succeeded in establishing and deepening the so-called Negative Theology, not only among the people of Israel but also among gentiles (e.g., Thomas Aquinas, the greatest Christian theologian and philosopher), which earned him recognition until this very day, "Which (God) has no body, and will not be attained by those in body and has no resemblance whatsoever". In this supreme spiritual effort, Maimonides succeeded in refining and purifying the faith of any deception of idolatry, that is to say, of everything within the realm of the creation. This is by showing that all the human attributes mentioned in relation to God, such as form, action, or any attribute, including spiritual ones, are nothing more than a human expression of something we cannot utter otherwise. Therefore, God cannot be described in any category imaginable by a human being.

This supreme sublimation of faith is undoubtedly the unique contribution of Judaism to the elevation of human theological thinking.

Appendix

The Ancient Near East

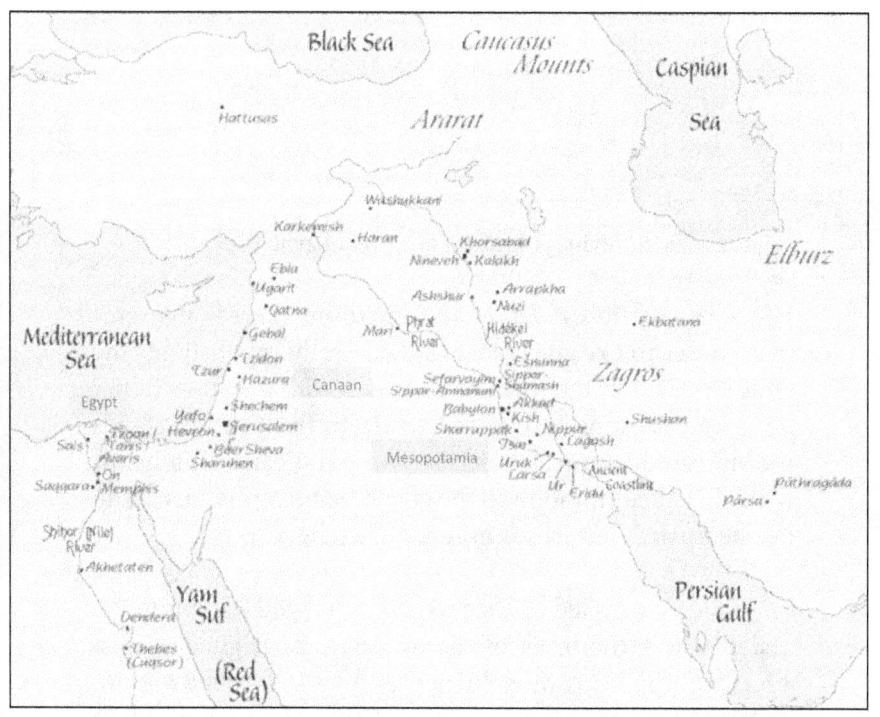

The Papyrus of Hor

Figure A.2: The divine judgement in ancient Egypt. Papyrus of Hor.

HERE, IN THE DIVINE Egyptian courtroom, there is an exemplary order to execute justice. Down on the right stands the goddess Maat in the form of a woman with a feather in her head, representing justice and truth. In front of her stands the deceased, the King's scribe Hor, who raises his hands with joy and admiration to the gods (compare: "Let us lift up our heart with our hands unto God." (Lam 3, 41)

Later, Hor is led by the jackal-headed god Anubis to the scales, where the heart of the deceased is weighed against a feather. The heart must be lighter than it, for its owner to be found righteous (i.e., cleansed of sin—since sin weighs a person's heart, "And Pharaoh hardened his heart [Hebrew—made it heavy]" (Exod 8:28). Interesting is the parallelism with the Book of Job, "Let me be weighed in a just balance, that God may know mine integrity." (Job 31, 6)

On the other side of the scale stands the Secretary of the Gods (with the head of the bird Ibis, its feathers used for writing), equipped with writing tools and a tablet for recording and reporting the results to the chief god Osiris, the ruler of the underworld, judge of the dead, and the god of resurrection.

On his left, a monstrous creature is kneeling on a small temple-like stand waiting patiently to devour the hearts that did not pass the test.

On the elevated throne sits the chief god Osiris, who holds government insignia (a crook and a flail), before him a table full of refreshments, a sacrifice on behalf of the deceased to appease him. Behind him in the gesture of admiration are the goddesses Isis and Nephthys, bare-breasted, as was the Egyptian fashion of those days. If the deceased is found righteous, he will be delivered by them to the Elysian fields, the final resting place of the souls (Paradise).

Chronicle

The expulsion of the Hyksos from Egypt—1550 BCE.

The Judges era—thirteenth century BCE, late Bronze Age.

The emergence of the kingdom of Israel—tenth century BCE.

The appearance of the kingdom of Judah—ninth century BCE.

Destruction of the kingdom of Israel and its capital Samaria by Shalmaneser V and Sargon III, kings of Assyria—721-722 BCE.

Destruction of the kingdom of Judah and its capital Jerusalem by Nebuchadnezzar II of Babylon—586 BC.

The order of the events

The beginning of the Babylonian conquest of the large Assyrian kingdom, 625 BCE, and the conquest of its capital Nineveh—612 BCE.

605 BCE, the famous Battle of Carchemish (see Jeremiah 41) on the Euphrates River in the north where Nebuchadnezzar II, king of Babylon, defeated the Egyptian army and took over the entire region of Canaan including Judah.

CHRONICLE

Jehoiakim king of Judah rebelled, and in 598 BCE Nebuchadnezzar occupied Jerusalem and exiled the king, his family, and the nobles of the people, and appointed his uncle Zedekiah king.

Zedekiah rebelled again, and in 586–587 BCE after a long siege Nebuchadnezzar conquered Jerusalem, destroyed the city with Solomon's Temple, and exiled the inhabitants to Babylon.

Bibliography

Amir, David. *Gods and Heroes: Canaanite plots found in Ugarit* (full translation of all Ugaritic poetry). Hakibbutz Hameuchad, Israel: Sifriat Poalim, 1987 [Hebrew].
Bahat, Dan. "Excavations at Tel Mardich," *Antiquities-Kadmoniot* 13 (1971): 32-29 [Hebrew].
Black, Jeremy A., Graham Cunningham, Eleanor Robson, and Gábor Zólyomi. *Inana and Bilulu: an ulila to Inana.* The Electronic Text Corpus of Sumerian Literature. Oxford: Oriental Institute, University of Oxford, 2016. http://etcsl.orinst.ox.ac.uk/
Black, Jeremy, and Anthony Green. *Gods, Demons and Symbols, of Ancient Mesopotamia.* London: The British Museum Press, 1992.
Bramet, Haim, and Michael Weizmenn. *Ebla—An Archeological Mystery.* Jerusalem: Keter, 1982.
Cassuto, Moshe Daviv. *Ha'ela Anat: Canaanite Plot Songs from the Age of the Patriarchs.* Jerusalem: Bialik Institute, 1951 [Hebrew].
Darshan, Nogah, and Gai Darshan. *Canaanite Mythology (Myths 15).* Tel-Aviv: Mapa, 2008 [Hebrew].
Ganan, Moshe. *Sumerian Poems.* Jerusalem: Goshen, 1970 [Hebrew].
Isserlin, Ben S.L. *The Israelites*, London: Thames & Hudson Ltd., 1998.
Kempinski, Aaron. "Tel Mardikh-Ebla, 1964-1978," *Qadmoniot* 12 (1979): 98-112 [Hebrew].
Klein, Yaacov, and Shin Shifra. *In Those Distant Days: An Anthology of Mesopotamian Literature.* Tel-Aviv: Am Oved, 1996 [Hebrew].
Kutscher, Rafael. "Corrections and Additions to the Article 'Ebla Documents' (Teudot Ebla)." *Qadmoniot* 127 (1980): 52-51 [Hebrew].
Kutscher, Rafael. "Ebla Documents (Teudot Ebla)." *Qadmoniot* 48 (1979): 121-113 [Hebrew].
Mitchell, Terence, C. *The Bible in the British Museum. Interpreting the Evidence.* London: The British Museum Press, 2001.
Reade, Julian. *Mesopotamia.* London: British Museum Press, 1991.
Rin, Zvi. *The Plots of the Gods.* Jerusalem: The Society for Biblical Research in Israel, 1968 [Hebrew].

BIBLIOGRAPHY

Robins, Gay. *The Art of Ancient Egypt*. London: The British Museum Press, 1997.
Sivan, Daniel. *Ugaritic Grammar*. Jerusalem: Bialik Institute, 1993 [Hebrew].
Tiradritti, Francesco. *Ancient Egypt*. London: The British Museum Press, 2002.
Tubb, Jonathan N. *Canaanites*. London: The British Museum Press, 1998.
Wallis Budge, E.A. *Egyptian Ideas of the Afterlife*. New York: Dover, 1995.

www.ingramcontent.com/pod-product-compliance
Lightning Source LLC
Chambersburg PA
CBHW070926160426
43193CB00011B/1587